Recycled WOMEN

COMPILED BY:

Rosemary Fisher & Kristin Jordan

Recycled Women LLC

PO Box 535

Columbia, TN 38402

Email: rosemary@recycledwomen.org

Website: www.recycledwomen.org

ISBN-13: 978-1461045311

ISBN-10: 1461045312

Compiled by Rosemary Fisher and Kristin Jordan

Printed in the United States of America

First printing 2011

DEDICATION

For Christine Petros who taught me how to love unconditionally by example...Thank you for never giving up on me!!
I miss and love you!

For Gary Clements who taught me "The devil knows who you are and he is afraid you are going to find out!"...
We miss and love you Gary!

CONTENTS

INTRODUCTION

I pray that this book encourages you to be ALL that God has called you to be regardless of your past circumstances or mistakes. I personally found so much freedom and power by hearing true life transforming testimonies from women just like me. Too many women are not living in victory because they are shackled by shame, fear, guilt, unforgiveness and bitterness.

I have good news! God is in the Recycling Business! He will take what man wants to throw in the trash and make useful for His Glory. Oh how fast we are to throw out things that we think have no value, including our gifts and talents because we believe a lie that was spoken over us or experienced an event we think we can't forgive or get over. It is time to shake those shackles off your feet!

This book contains stories of women from all ages, different denominational backgrounds and life circumstances. The enemy attacked and tried to stop these ladies from reaching their divine destinies only to be halted by their willingness to surrender to the power of Almighty God. These ladies took their mess and turned it into a beautiful message to encourage you that regardless of your past mistakes you can also be an overcomer and have a life worth living! If you are a Christ follower it is time to walk in victory. Jesus already paid the price and the time to WIN is now!

If you don't know Christ Jesus as your personal Lord and Savior, I pray after you read these stories that your heart be open to ask Him to take your life and make it brand new! I have included a simple prayer at the back of the book along with biblical scriptures to get you started on a brand new life.

Remember, it doesn't matter how you start, it only matters how you finish. I pray that these testimonies will be the beginning of you having the spirit of boldness to start sharing your victories and stories to give God ALL the glory that He deserves to help someone else. We would love to hear from you and pray that you will keep in touch and tell us how these stories have impacted your life.

Blessings in Abundance,

Rosemary Fisher
Founder, Recycled Women Ministries
www.recycledwomen.org

ACKNOWLEDGMENTS

Thank you to my amazing husband Rick who is always encouraging me to be all that God wants me to be and seeking God's wisdom for leading our family! You are a spiritual giant and I thank God for you. He has truly given me beauty for ashes and I am so blessed to call you "My Gift from God"!

Thank you to my very creative and talented son, Beau. You are a constant reminder of God's grace and unconditional love. You make my heart sing and I love you!

Thank you to my sweet friend and spiritual sister, Kristin Jordan who heard and saw the vision of this ministry five years ago! Thank you for your powerful prayers, your assistance in gathering stories and always keeping me accountable to the vision God gave me. You are amazing and I love and adore you! I also want to thank your Godly husband Montell and your children Christopher, Sydney and Skyler for always supporting you and me during this incredible journey and allowing you to travel and spend time building this ministry. They gave so much up to watch you soar in your gift and I am forever grateful!

A special thank you to George and Margaret Heard for always bringing such joy and smiles in my life! Thank you for being such powerful prayer warriors and having such a servant's heart for Jesus Christ. Margaret, you are my inspiration and your smile is contagious. Thank you for always going the extra mile to encourage me to get this done. I am such a blessed woman to have you in my life! I love you girlfriend!

Thank you to all my sweet Recycled Women authors who are willing to walk unashamed from their past to help others experience freedom through your transparent and honest stories. I look forward to touring and spreading this message around the world with each of you! I love you!

A special thank you to Dianne Baker and Sarah Willems for editing the stories and giving me lots of encouragement and patience through this project. You both are talented, amazing and such Godly women! Thank you for being my Spiritual Moms! I am so BLESSED!

Thank you Barrie Taylor for your amazing photographs and your willingness to go "Above and Beyond" in your creative work to please our Lord and Savior Jesus Christ!

A lifelong thank you to Todd and Donna Cash for being my first Christian spiritual mentors and teaching me what a Godly Christian life looks like! You have no idea how much I value the time we have spent together and how I cherish the encouragement you always gave me to become all that God made me to be. I love you!!

Thank you to Matt LaMey from www.designsbylemay.com for coming to our rescue at such short notice to create our Recycled Women logo for the cover of this book! I pray that God bless you with an abundance of work!

Thank you John Griffin, Publisher of Christian Living Magazine for allowing me to work by your side over the years! You have taught me how to take a vision and listen for God's sweet voice. You are the best example of how to run a ministry or a large corporation by always believing in your team and your willingness to do whatever it takes to get the job done! You are the brother I always prayed for and our family loves and appreciates you!

A special shout out of love to my Recycled Women Ministry Team (Margaret Heard, Suzanne Gagneur, Peggy Clements, Ashley Holt, Rev. Dustin Laster and Rev. Guy and Becky Yeager)! Your dedication to this ministry is priceless and I love you.

Thank you Karen Ford, Michael and Christopher Bratta from isXperia for helping get this project off the ground! Thank you for believing in me and this ministry!

Thank you Blake Hight for your willingness to read the stories even though you did not fit our demographic profile to give us your young adult male feedback! Your encouragement was priceless!

A special thank you to Dr. Dale Ledbetter and the Maury Baptist Association for showing me that unity does exist in the body of Christ. I thank you for allowing me to serve you these past four years.

And finally, a very special thank you to Rev. Eric Nichols for being such a wonderful blessing to each of us Recycled Women! Your love for the Lord is contagious and you walk the walk! Thank you for always challenging us to draw closer to our Lord and Savior. A special thank you to your beautiful "Super Model" wife, Beth and your three children Ashleigh, Morgan and Daniel for sacrificing time with their daddy to spend time ministering to us ladies. May God continue to chase you all down with blessings and favor!

A Beautiful Recycled Woman

By Sonjalyn

Recycled Women ... at first I didn't like that term. It conjured up images of disappointed dads, angry boyfriends, and disenchanted husbands lined up at the recycling center waiting their turn to have their "woman" recycled. I felt hurt, disappointed, and dehumanized. Those feelings, however, were quickly replaced by excitement when I discovered my own meaning for *Recycled Women*. It happened while I created invitations to a bridesmaids' tea for my niece.

I found the most wonderful art paper for those invitations ... recycled art paper. And it was perfect! As I worked with that unique paper, it all became quite clear to me. *Recycled Women*, like that recycled art paper, are not women who have been "traded in" for something better. No! Each and every piece of our former lives—each page of our individual stories—has been artfully transformed, reformed, and recreated into something exceptional ... something extraordinary ... something beautiful.

At first glance, the recycled art paper I worked with was creamy, beige, and mundane. But when I looked closer, I discovered the beauty. Each sheet contained thousands of subtle colors and shapes. Each had a unique texture and weight. Each sheet of recycled art paper was an individual work of art.

Like the recycled art paper, recycled women are distinctive. Each one is filled with thousands of small, intricate, and unique parts that make the whole woman. Each recycled woman has her stories, her goals, her passions, her dreams. We are disfigured, flawed, and imperfect, but it is our imperfections that make us rare beauties!

I was born into an exceptionally warm and loving Christian family. My dad was a southern gentleman, and my mother was a perfect lady. It was fascinating growing up during the 1960s and '70s in Florida. Daddy worked for NASA on the Mercury, Gemini, and Apollo projects and Momma worked for the Chamber of Commerce. Life was an adventure; but I had my fears. America was in the midst of the cold war, and we routinely participated in bomb and fallout drills. Daddy had a bomb shelter built in the backyard, and Momma kept survival kits for all of us, even for the pets.

I learned to shoot before I started kindergarten and could speak at least some Spanish. I, the oldest of four children, was the adventurer, the rule breaker, the one that questioned everything, and the humanitarian. I knew with certainty that it could all end any day! As a result, I developed an unquenchable thirst for life—an atypical need to experience everything life had to offer and an overwhelming need to nurture and protect those weaker or less fortunate than I was. Those traits have brought me indescribable pain, as well as unimaginable pleasure.

One Christmas, we gathered around the tree to open our gifts, and Momma began to read off the names attached to each package and stocking. When all the gifts and stockings had been distributed, I had none ... nothing ... not even fruit in my stocking. My younger siblings were concerned and tried to comfort me. I remember telling them, "I'm ok. I know why I didn't get anything from Santa. It's because I'm too old, and I don't believe in him anymore."

I remember that Momma and Daddy offered no comfort, but asked me to come help them in the kitchen. I walked to the kitchen to help Momma with breakfast, and Daddy asked me to take the trash out. When I walked out the back door with the trash bag in my hand, there stood my grandparents next to their car. My grandmother had something in her hand ... a bridle! Grandmother Cecil was holding a bridle with a big red bow tied to it!

"Jump in baby," Granddaddy John hollered!

The whole family rode out to a friend's farm, and there he stood. To my momma he was a dangerous wild beast ... a menace to her family ... a mighty and imposing force ... but to me he was an un-tamed beauty ... terrified, anxious, and abandoned. I ran to him, and suddenly my family, the fences, the whole world were swallowed up in a great abyss. There was nothing on earth except us—me and my beautiful wild mustang, Frisky. He needed me! I knew he needed me.

He was everything I had ever wanted. He was an adventure to be had ... a handsome renegade, wild and untamed. He knew no rules and respected no boundaries, and yet there he was, abandoned and frightened. Yes, he needed me!

Several years later, my friends and I were laughing, joking, and eating too much pizza ... doing what teenage girls do, when from across the room I saw him. He was tall, muscular, and athletic, and he was staring directly at me. With long blond curls that framed his face like a lion's mane and dressed in black like a gunfighter in a Clint Eastwood movie, he crossed the room toward me. As he came, I sensed he was dangerous and a menace. I felt his imposing strength ... but I also saw that he was a beautiful and arresting beast. When he reached me, he kissed me! Just walked up, leaned across the table, took my face in his hand, bent down, and kissed me. I instantly knew he needed me!

Our marriage lasted almost six years. Six years of turmoil and turbulence ... six years of disappointment and distress ... six years of abuse, neglect, fear, and humiliation. From the beginning, he took ev-erything he wanted—all that I had—and he gave nothing in return. From the beginning, he never apologized. Why should he apologize? It was always my fault. I made him angry. I didn't try hard enough. I was too emotional, unreasonable, ignorant, and just plain stupid! I was distant, frigid, and the worst sin of all, I had let myself go!

Whenever he beat me, he would stand over me and say, "Go, leave, take your stuff and get out ... but no one will want you. You will be alone. You're worthless. You're not worth the price of the bullet it would take to put you out of your misery." He would then storm out of the house until his money was gone and he needed clean clothes; then he would come back. Back to me ... because he needed me!

I didn't leave him, but one night he just walked into our home and told me to get out. He said he had filed for divorce and was keeping everything. "Take the kid and go to your momma's," he said. "They still love you, but I want you out of my house!" He threw our child and me out just like trash thrown along a highway.

By the time our divorce was final, I didn't recognize myself. I weighed a little over 300 pounds, my hair was prematurely gray, and I was filled with hatred. I was filled with the self-loathing type of hatred that fills every fiber of one's being. I was lost. The adventurer, the rule breaker, the one that had questioned everything, the humanitarian was all gone ... and what was left was a tired, bitter old woman. I couldn't even cry. I had no tears left. All I had was hatred.

Hate was my companion until something miraculous happened! I began to talk to God. Well, to be honest, I began to question God. On one particular day, I was sitting out at the end of a long dock watching the day turn to night, and I was asking, "Why me? What did I do?"

When I looked down, I saw a snake under the dock. It was a coral snake—small and beautiful, but deadly! I remembered an old story. Some say it is a Native American tale; others say it is a tale from Africa brought over by slaves. I don't know where the tale originated, but it was what I needed to remember, and God knew it. God used that beautiful, venomous little serpent to help me find my way home.

The tale goes something like this: A child finds a beautiful snake. The snake is cold and hungry and asks the child to help him. The child knows the snake is venomous, but it is beautiful, and it is asking for help. The snake needs the child, so the child helps the snake. By the end of the tale, the snake has taken everything from the child—his home, his family, his friends. Finally, the snake bites the child and leaves him to die. When the child cries, "Why?" the snake offers no apology, but says, "You knew I was a snake when you brought me into your home."

At that moment, I experienced an epiphany—a comprehension of reality by means of a sudden intuitive realization. I knew God had not hurt me and He had not filled me with hatred. So, I could stop hating my ex-husband. My ex-husband had not locked me in a cell; he had not forced me to stay and endure his wrath. I had made my own choice to stay.

I had known what he was like before I had married him. I knew what he was before I dated him. I knew what he was before I let him kiss me. I had allowed this to happen because I thought he needed me. I had given him all of me, everything I was, and he was not worthy of that gift.

My eyes were opened, and by the grace of God, I had been saved! Saved in every since of the word. And I was free. I was free to live and to love ... I was free once again to seek adventure, to break the rules, to question everything except God's love, and to be a humanitarian.

When I got home, I sat down and made a list ... a list of goals. And I began to work on those goals. I still have my list. It is a work in progress, a living entity. My list is constantly growing and changing, but it is "My" list. And the number one, unchangeable, constant on the list is pray: pray for forgiveness, pray for healing, and pray for opportunities to help others. I also thank God every day for everyone and everything in my life.

Let me assure you, God hears and answers prayers! I've been led to serve on several active committees and boards; driven to champion unpopular causes; and provoked into alliance with the "underdog"! The most challenging task; however, comes on occasions when I find my hands and my tongue tied. On these rare occasions I know God. I feel God. God holds me; keeps me still; allows me to linger; take note; to just be there!

I now possess an unquenchable thirst for life—an atypical need to experience everything life has to offer and an overwhelming need to nurture and protect those weaker or less fortunate than I. Those traits have brought me indescribable pain, as well as unimaginable pleasure ... but I have my story, my goals, my passions, and my dreams. I am disfigured, flawed, and imperfect, but it is those imperfections that make me a rare and beautiful "Recycled Woman."

Due to the direct link between animal neglect and cruelty and violent crime including domestic violence, Sonjalyn is an advocate for neglected and abused pets. In Sonjalyn's spare time, she lobbies changing laws within the State making animal neglect and abuse a felony with minimum sentences and fines. Proverbs 12:10 (NLT) says: *The godly care for their animals, but the wicked are always cruel.*

Life is like a Box of Chocolates

By Suzanne

I grew up in California with an older brother and a younger sister. Others saw our family as a typical happy family. My dad was a pilot and traveled internationally while my mother stayed at home to raise us. What a lot of people did not see, however, was that my fifteen-year-old brother was a drug addict and both of my parents were alcoholics. My father traveled and was gone for days at a time. When he was gone, my mother drank more often. She drank early every evening and then fell asleep on the sofa. Consequently, I became very independent at a young age.

My grandmother took me to church because my family did not often attend. I came to know Christ and was saved and baptized at the age of twelve. Shortly after that, we moved to Tennessee, where I met a friend whose family regularly attended church. I never really had any spiritual growth after accepting Christ other than watching my grandmother and my friend and her family and the way they lived their lives.

My grandmother read her Bible every night before bed. She also told me stories of how God had helped her through the hard struggles in her life as she had grown up and had by herself raised my dad and my uncle, who had Muscular Dystrophy. Every time I was at my friend's house, I went to church with her and her family. Her house became a "home away from home" for me and I stayed there a lot.

I fell away from God as I grew into my teenage years. In high school, I met a guy who would later become my husband. We became friends and dated for about a year. I graduated at eighteen and was married to him six months later.

The first few months of our marriage were great, but then I noticed my newlywed husband would often not come to bed. When I asked him why, he would say he just fell asleep on the sofa. This continued night after night and when I approached him about it, he just made up a lot of excuses. He was also not as affectionate as when we first were married, and I had begun to ask myself why? At the age of 19, after being married just a few months, I became pregnant with a beautiful daughter.

Since this was my first marriage and serious relationship, when I saw the change in my husband's behavior, I thought the problem was that I was doing something wrong or not doing something that I needed to do to please him. I had several things running through my head, but since I had no one to talk with, I kept it all to myself. I told myself to just take it for what it was. Our relationship was good, and we got along great. But I still wondered why my husband did not want to make love to his new wife?

After being married a little over a year, I came home early from work one night and discovered why our marriage had changed. I walked in on my husband with ANOTHER MAN. I felt as if my whole world had just collapsed. As my husband walked towards me to explain, I physically picked him up, carried him out of our trailer, and threw him out in our front yard.

This all happened during the holiday season, and I did not want to ruin the Christmas spirit, but all I could think about was, *"What am I going to do? How am I going to tell my family, friends, and coworkers that my husband is gay? What would they think? How would they react; and how could I have been so blind to all of it?*

I had not talked much with God during my earlier years, but I developed a strong yearning for Him. I prayed, *"Please God, help me!"*

I asked myself many questions. *Can I make this marriage work? How did I fail? What could I have done differently?* I had planned on being married only once in my life.

I felt the situation was my fault for not seeing any signs of my husband's problem. My husband said he could not change the way he felt inside. He said he had thought being married to a woman would help him change, but he had found out that he was wrong.

I found myself alone at the age of twenty-one with the responsibility of caring for an infant child. I was not close to my family, and they did not help me or watch my daughter while she was growing up. I loved my family, but I just could not talk with them about life issues ... so I just kept to myself.

As I look back now, I see that even though I was not completely in God's will and did not have a close relationship with Him, He was still there guiding me and loving me. I am not sure why God allows us to be put in certain situations, trials, and troubles, but I believe it brought me back a little closer to Him.

A year later, my daughter and I were still on our own, but I met a gentleman at work and we connected right away. We talked often but never went out on a date. He told me that he was separated from his wife and getting a divorce, and I believed him. We began seeing each other and had strong feelings for one another. However, after a few months of happy bliss, I found out that he was not divorced but was separating from his wife. I told him he had to get a divorce or I was gone.

He chose me, and I thought that was great, but once again, as I look back on this situation, I should have seen the warning signs—but I was weak. He would call and say something had come up and we couldn't go out that evening. Then he became more cautious about our relationship. It was when he said that it would be better if he called me and that I should not call his house that the flags went up, and I questioned him about his ex-wife. Yes, I should have left then, but I had strong feelings for him and wanted our relationship to work.

After a few months had passed, his ex-wife called and said she was going to have his child. Once again, I was devastated but was determined to stand by my man. Several months later, we were married. I was twenty-three years old.

Everything seemed to be going well with our marriage. My new husband and daughter got along, my stepdaughter from his previous marriage was born and we were happy. After two years of marriage my husband had to have another open heart surgery. He had his first heart surgery three years before we were married.

It was very hard to see my husband go through that type of surgery and not know what the outcome would be. The doctors said that anything could happen: his heart could stop during surgery, or he could have a stroke on the table. All I could do was pray that God would keep him safe.

Seven years into our marriage, I found pictures in his car of him with a coworker. She was posing nude and found out that he had been having an affair with her for a year. This hurt brought back many of the same feelings I had experienced with my first husband and was devastated.

The same old questions came back to haunt me. *What did I do? Not do? Was I not good enough for him? God, what is wrong with me?*

This time, my husband and I tried to work things out. I gave him the choice to either choose her or choose me. He chose me, but because of the affair, I really did not trust him. I had a hard time forgiving, let alone forgetting. I just could not get passed the hurt and deception. Although we stayed married for three more rocky years, I felt empty inside.

My husband suffered a massive heart attack and I found him on the floor of our living room early one morning. He was still alive when I got to him and called an ambulance. By the time I arrived at the hospital, he had died. My world, needless to say, had collapsed once again. *How do I tell the kids? How do I tell his parents? Why did this have to happen?* I was in shock, and the following few days were just a blur. I had never had to bury anyone before.

To this day, I still battle guilt because the night before he died, we'd had an argument, and he had stayed up and not come to bed. The guilt of that argument, along with the "what ifs" that replay in my mind has been unbearable. What if he'd been in bed with me and I had heard him call? Maybe, just maybe, I could have helped him, and he would still be alive today. I know he knew that I loved him, but it was still hard not being able to say that last, *"I'm sorry"*. I hated that he had left this world with us fighting.

On the day of the funeral, a pastor from my friend's church came to the funeral home and wanted to pray with me. I did not even know this man, but as he began to pray with me, I cannot even begin to describe the huge opening up of my heart that I felt. Even though I was going through one of the most difficult times I had ever been through, I knew without a shadow of a doubt that God showed up through this Pastor on that significant day of my life because I had such peace come over me. Most of the funeral was a blur, but that moment will forever be imprinted on my heart and imbedded in my mind.

A few weeks after my husband had passed away, I had a vision that he came to me and stood at the foot of my bed and told me that everything would be ok. I don't know why he visited me except for the fact that I needed closure in my heart that he was ok. I believe God sent him back to me to give me that inner peace I needed.

In January 1995, I rededicated my life to the Lord and my daughter was baptized that same day. Soon after that, I met the man that would be the love of my life. I had actually known him and his partner from work for a few years through the company we both worked for.

A few months after my husband's passing, he came into my office to talk. We had never really talked much other than in passing, but this day was different. By the time he left my office, he had asked me out for a date. I had not been asked out for a date in over 10 years, and it was definitely a weird feeling. I reluctantly said "yes."

In my eyes this was not a date but a meeting to see if I liked him and if we had anything in common. After about two weeks, I agreed to meet him at a local restaurant. I was never really one to date and with two failed marriages under my belt I was a little gun shy and scared to say the least. We began dating and had a lot in common, we enjoyed each others company. He had come out of a bad divorce a few years prior after being married over 15 years. He had 2 children and I had one. Everyone seemed to hit it off great.

Before making a commitment, I analyzed my past two marriages and our relationships to see what I may have done or what I could change about myself. It took a while, but what I found was that I had no control over how they ended. In other words, my marriages failed because of choices. One chose to be gay and said he could not change. The other chose to have an affair and he told me it was nothing I had done and although he loved me, he was attracted to other women. We cannot control other people, we can only control our own choices and to pay attention to what and who our choices are going to affect. God wants us to strive, work on being more like Christ every day. We should want to show others what God has done for us, even more so during our trials and troubles. Through these experiences, God has shown me that I cannot control what other people do or say.

Me and my new friend became best friends over the next 1-½ years. During this time we started attending church. I no longer wanted to control my life and wanted God to control everything, so I rededicated my life and was baptized. It was an awesome day!

Two years after dating, we married and started feeling led to hear more about mission trips. I love to help people, but felt that a mission trip may be out of my comfort zone and was not sure about it. We prayed and in 2003, we had the chance to go on a local mission trip. It was the most awesome, exciting trip we had ever taken. We were both hooked and have been on several mission trips to different areas, local and out of state ever since. We met new friends, helped people that truly needed help and showed them we do all of this because we love the Lord and that the Lord loves them. It is such a great feeling to tell someone that our help does not cost them a thing and it is all done with and through the love of Christ.

I know now that God was there all those years watching me try to do it all by myself. I was the one that chose to move out of His will. I am so thankful for His grace and mercy. I know God has great things for my life, and all I have to do is open my heart and mind to listen and receive His message. Having an open heart will always mean I can receive His love and give it to others.

I look back on all my trials and not having God as my foundation in my life and realize it was hard to handle those times alone. But now I have God as my rock. I still have trials and hard times, but I know I have someone to talk to and to pray to. Just knowing of His grace and how He died to save me has given me a relationship with God that gives me peace.

I thank God every day that He is there for me and that I do not have to deal or handle my problems for myself. Knowing and believing that I have a God that loves me more than anything and that He is there for me at ALL times, gives me such comfort.

Proverbs 3:5 (NKJV) says, *"Trust in the Lord with all your heart, and lean not on your own understanding."* God is my strength and I am a Daughter of the King!

All Sufficient Grace

By Tammy Barrett

The year 2000 began without a hitch. My husband and I had moved our family in July to Iowa—the Quad-cities. It had been a big decision, as we were living out of our home state for the first time in our lives, but our business had grown in Iowa and had great potential if given personal attention. We had reasoned that our boys were young enough to make the move without much trouble.

We had worked through most of the difficult transitions and life had settled into a routine. The boys had made friends, we had found a church home, and we had survived what everyone kept telling us was a mild winter—even though it was unlike any we had ever seen. I was attending Bible Study Fellowship and meeting new ladies, I had found a doctor and gotten insurance.

Finding a doctor and getting insurance had been major, since right before we moved I had gone to an ENT to have my left ear checked because I was having trouble hearing thinking I had some hardened wax in my ear. The doctor had run tests and had called me back on the day we were loading the U-Haul to move to Iowa. He told me I had a small benign tumor that needed to be removed, but it wasn't life threatening. He advised me to get a second opinion when we got settled in Iowa.

We moved in July, and it took until November to get our group coverage changed to an Iowa plan. It was a huge miracle that the Iowa plan had accepted me because I had received a Lupus diagnosis, as well as the diagnosis of the tumor.

When I saw my new doctor, he was a little more urgent and concerned than the first doctor. He sent me to a specialist who explained that while the tumor was most likely benign, it had to be removed because it was on the acoustic nerve which was up against my brain stem. He could not believe I wasn't having problems with balance and speech. The amazing thing was that this doctor specialized in the particular kind of surgery I needed—ten hour brain surgery.

After we got home, my husband researched the diagnosis on the Internet. We wanted to know: Was this surgery common? Was surgery the only way? Who was this surgeon I had seen anyway? We not only found out about the type of tumor I had and the surgery, but we also found out that my surgeon was one of the top two surgeons in the nation for this kind of tumor! If I had still lived in Oklahoma, such surgery would not have been available. God had placed us just forty-five minutes away from one of the best surgeons in the nation!

The surgeon explained to us that the safest procedure—the procedure with the least trauma to the brain—would be to enter my skull through my left ear canal. This method, however, would require removing everything in my inner ear and would result in total hearing loss in that ear. I had already lost about sixty percent of my hearing in that ear due to the tumor, so it was an easy decision.

The surgeon also explained that I would experience paralysis of the left side of my face—much like a stroke victim experiences—and also balance and vision problems until everything healed. The recovery time would be a minimum of six to eight weeks, and the effects would be felt for a lifetime.

I called to talk to my mom about my upcoming surgery and plans for my boys. She was a strong believer in healing and did not want me to have to go through the surgery. I told her, however, that I had peace, and that whatever God chose to do—heal me or carry me through the surgery—was okay, and I wasn't afraid. Mom then agreed to take some of her vacation time and come to stay with the boys, which relieved my biggest concern.

The next day, a phone call from my brother came that changed everything. I answered the call, but he asked to speak to my husband.

I could tell he didn't have good news, but I never dreamed just how bad the news was. When he hung up, he told me my mom had collapsed at work and was in the emergency room. They thought she'd had a heart attack, but they weren't sure yet.

A heart attack! Are you kidding me? My mom was never sick, took no regular meds, and was only fifty-three years old. However, I knew she had been under a lot of stress, because my brother had been in some trouble. Since Mom had divorced my stepdad, it had been just my mom and my brother. *Stress had to be the reason.*

My mind raced. I'd go take care of her, that's all she needed. A little rest and a little time off and she'd be as good as new. I'd always wanted to be able to retire her, and maybe now our business would allow it.

We called our pastor, and he came and prayed and stayed with us. Finally, I couldn't wait any longer. I called the emergency room and asked for the family. My grandma came on the line and wasn't holding it together very well. This was "Nanna," a nurse for thirty or more years. Nothing shook her. I didn't remember ever seeing her "lose it."

"Tammy," she said, "I don't know if they are going to be able to do anything!"

"What are you talking about?" I said. "She's young; it's a heart attack; of course they can do something!"

"There is so much blood, and they have lost her twice already," Nanna said. "It doesn't look good!"

"I'm on my way!" I replied.

I hung up and dialed the airlines while my husband picked up the boys from school. I bought tickets, packed, and soon headed to the airport. I kept thinking that if I got there in time everything would be OK. *Oh why had I moved so far away?*

There was a long lay-over in St. Louis, so I called Mom's house. I knew they would still be at the hospital, but I just wanted to leave a message and let them know that I was on my way when my brother answered the phone. *Why wasn't he at the hospital with mom?* I wondered.

"Tammy, I'm sorry," he said.

"I'm coming as quick as I can," I told him.

And just like that, in the middle of the St. Louis Airport, I learned that my beautiful, strong, mother had died of an aortal aneurism. I felt as though someone or something had ripped a piece of flesh from my heart, never to be returned. I felt physical pain that was unbearable.

I'd grown up without my dad, and even after I'd had a stepdad, my mom had been the center of my universe—my anchor—the strongest person I knew. The ache was crushing. I hadn't gotten there in time. I hadn't gotten to say goodbye.

The next days and weeks went by in a blur of people and decisions, with eyes always looking and checking to see if I was making it. I wanted to go to bed and never get up; never answer another question; never think another "what-if." The only thing that kept me putting one foot in front of the other was my boys. I never wanted them to know such pain, the pain of not having a mother.

I cried out to God. How could I cope? I didn't have much time to grieve. Even though the wound was raw, I had another battle to wage. My surgery was less than six weeks away.

I pleaded with my brother to leave everything just like it was and give me some time: time to have surgery, time to heal, and time to come back and wade through all of Mom's things.

I flew back to Iowa with my family and I clung to them, feeling like they were all I had left in the world. My brain seemed to switch to autopilot. I had to be okay for my boys and I had to be a strong woman of faith like my mom.

I talked to the boys about my surgery and assured them everything would be fine. We prayed, and I asked them to pray. I shared scripture. They were little prayer warriors, and their faith was childlike—perfect, without doubt or fear.

I attended Bible Study Fellowship and dug into the word. I approached my surgery very matter-of-factly. I made plans for the boys; I bought plane tickets for my grandparents; and I took a step of faith and shared what was happening with the strangers in my Bible Study. I say strangers because I'd only known them for a few short months and only in a formal setting; but I needed someone else to pray because my prayer warrior, my strength, my mom, was gone.

Once again, God was there with a miracle. The lady to my right said, *"My father-in-law just went through that very same surgery. I can tell you what to expect, and we'll get through this."* Those ladies who barely knew me became Christ's arms and hands in the next weeks, caring for us like family. Our business associates, and now dear friends, in Iowa sprang into action with offers to keep the kids, pray, and prepare food. One dear friend offered to be there the morning I went in for pre-op.

Letters and phone calls came from all across the country as people we did business with offered their encouragement. I could feel God's arms around us. We moved forward in faith, but in the quiet when I was alone, I cried out to God saying, *"I'm sick, and I need my mom. I can't do this ten hour surgery without her ... and what about my boys, God? No one knows them and loves them like my mom did. Why, God?"* And in my darkest hour, I told my husband, "I can't do this; I'm not strong enough!"

But then God made Himself known through a friend—my best friend, Donna, who called from Oklahoma. We had been best friends for over ten years, ever since we'd married best friends. We'd had our kids just months apart and had raised them together until we moved. Donna knew my boys and loved them like I did. She was God's answer to my cry. She told me she would be there the day of my surgery and would stay until I came home. I knew my boys wouldn't miss a beat. Donna would do soccer, little league, and car pool. She would read at bedtime and make breakfast in the morning.

God is so faithful! I knew I could do this in Him. I claimed a favorite scripture, 2 Corinthians 12:9 which says, *"My grace is sufficient for thee; for my strength is made perfect in weakness. Most gladly therefore will I rather glory in my infirmities, that the power of Christ may rest upon me."* (KJV)

Both of our boys were to have their birthdays while I was in the hospital, so my husband and I planned to give them their presents the morning I went to the hospital to help distract them. They would wake up that morning to bicycles and golf clubs.

The day of the surgery was finally here and I knew people were praying. Charlie Ragus, Founder of Advocare International, the company we moved out of State to help build, offered to come and wait with my husband during our time of need. Charlie organized a twenty-four-hour prayer chain where people across the nation were covering me and my family in prayer during surgery. Many of those people later told me they had never been a part of corporate prayer before and how much they were honored to be part of praying for me and my family. God was using this trial not only to build our faith, but also to build the faith and prayer life of hundreds of people all over the nation.

For ten long hours, my husband waited with my grandparents. Finally, the news came that the surgery was over and the tumor had been removed ... but the measure of success would not be known until I was alert enough for them to check to see if there had been any permanent damage to the acoustic nerve. The test would be to see if I could smile and raise my left eyebrow.

I awoke in darkness except for the soft flash of machines. I was in bed, but it was slanted to an almost upright position. I was strapped to the bed, and my head was in some kind of brace or helmet. I couldn't move a muscle. The nurse told me to try not to move; that it was important that I be very still.

The doctor came in and asked me to smile and try to raise my left eyebrow. I did both! He was excited and said that meant there was no permanent damage to the nerve. He brought my husband in and asked me to do those same things for him. I could see relief wash over my husband's face after his difficult ten hour wait.

I was so afraid and so alone, and I couldn't even call out. So I called out in my soul. I called out to Jesus and said, "*I know perfect love casts out all fear, and I need your perfect love now, here with me.*" Then Jesus came. I can't explain how I knew. I didn't see Him or hear Him, but I know beyond a shadow of a doubt that He came that night and sat at the end of my bed and ministered His perfect peace to me in my most profound darkness. He was there. I will never forget that night when His grace *was* sufficient, when His perfect love *did* cast out fear. I draw strength from it still.

I had a long, but victorious, recovery, and although I have not regained hearing in my left ear, I know that I know, that I know that God is real and that He is enough, no matter how big the need. I know that no matter how bad the hurt, His grace *is* sufficient, and that it is in our weakness that Christ is able to show Himself strong.

From the Pit to the Palace

By Dede

I was raised in a church where I witnessed a lot of hypocrisy and for lack of a better word...theatrics. I never learned of the loving, caring, forgiving side of Christ. I was taught the fire and brimstone, burning in Hell version. My church taught me that I was going to have to earn God's love and the salvation of my soul. That was too much pressure for a 13-year-old girl who was experiencing hormonal surges and peer pressure while being influenced by the magazine covers of "*Seventeen,*" "*Teen*" and "*Cosmopolitan*". To me, God didn't seem to fit into a normal person's life—unless of course you were a nun.

In college I worked while carrying a full academic load. I also went full time into the dating scene. It wasn't long until I tired of being used and abused by men who displayed no commitment, emotion or relationship. I decided it was my turn to take a predator's attitude when dating, a "get-them-before-they-get-you" approach. That way I would not get hurt. As an "empowered woman" I could chart my own course. I clubbed, partied and drank, all in the name of not being used anymore. Loose sex led to multiple abortions and an addiction to pornography and masturbation, which plagued me for years.

In my business writing class during my junior year of college, I met an amazingly funny, sexy guy. He was part Haitian and part Puerto Rican. I knew his step-father was a well known voodoo priest, but this didn't bother me.

The first time I met his family, his step-father (the voodoo priest) told me the date and the manner in which I was going to die. During that time in my life, I was afraid of death and because of this fear, I didn't even attend my grandmother's funeral the previous year.

With this new information regarding my fear of death, I became open to the proposed recommendations his step-father offered. We flew to New York City two weeks later so I could have a few rituals performed on me by his step-father. First recommendation was for me to have my spirit cleansed by spending some time sleeping in a coffin. (I don't know why my common sense never kicked in, but it didn't until it was too late!)

During the first and last ritual performed on me, I was sexually assaulted for four hours by my boyfriend's 350 pound step-father in the basement of his home while my boyfriend was one floor overhead watching television. I was sodomized and raped numerous times in a dark back room on a cold tile floor. My only defense was to emotionally remove myself from what was being done to me.

After the ordeal, I immediately told my boyfriend what had happened. He said he already knew and the rituals were the only way to 'save' me. He also told me that he loved me even more because of my willingness to submit to these horrible rituals. My body was badly lacerated while my wounded spirit slipped deeper into darkness.

Once I graduated from college, the results of those years fell hard upon me. After all the sex, drugs, and the complete disregard for my life or anyone else's, I had become addicted to a laundry list of prescription drugs, which I took for my numerous emotional issues— depression, anxiety, etc. Those issues left me sleepless and with a host of other physical problems.

My doctor continued to write prescriptions for each new complaint, and I couldn't function without a cocktail of three or more drugs in my system on a daily basis. All those years of partying and trying to out-do the hardest guys, left me emotionally bankrupt and empty.

I tried to kill myself dozens of times, but my medications only upset my stomach even more when I tried to overdose. I tried to kill myself because I could not deal with the faces and the memories that haunted my every waking moment. I had experienced far too many things in the years I had been drinking and bingeing on prescription drugs.

I remember standing in my shower one time, fully clothed, with the water running across my face just trying to escape how filthy I felt. I couldn't sleep at night because the faces of all the men I had slept with—both consensually and without my consent—would flash before my eyes. Whenever I was able to sleep, I would wake violently, in a cold sweat, shaking, and wondering if the things I had just seen in my mind were a reality or just nightmares.

Suicide became my only logical answer. Death, I thought, would finally quiet the voices in my head, the visions in my mind, and the memories burned into my flesh. Whenever I tried to kill myself, I would think, *Why do it anyway; no one loves you, so no one will even care that you're dead.* I believed at the time that I had no recourse for all the misery I was living through.

In all my misery and lonesomeness, I figured, *maybe, if I had a man I'd be better.* Well, if being unequally yoked, sexually active, sometimes physically and verbally abused, living with a voracious porn addiction and masturbating in order to cope was this so called "better" I was in search of was the answer, I was doing GREAT ... So great that I constantly cried myself to sleep.

I believed that my only remaining commodity of any worth was sex. A backward glance, even to my high school years revealed a warped value system: My self-esteem was directly connected to my success in the sexual manipulation of men. This was in direct contrast to all the values and expectations I learned at home and at church. My parents did their best to steer me in the right direction, but I was totally closed to their best guidance.

I left my parents' safe, secure home with its boundaries and guidance to move into a crime ridden urban area with a night-life. My life, my choices, and my decisions, right? Wrong ... so very, very wrong about everything I 'thought' I knew. I knew nothing, and my life was spiraling out of control.

A few more bad turns happened in my life, but through them all, something inside me kept saying "just go back to church." Remember,

I was raised in a church that had given me only a dry, religious, fire-and-brimstone memory of God and the church. Through each and every tragedy, every sleepless night, all the tears I cried, and all the tantrums I threw, God just kept talking to me—even though I wasn't ready to listen.

God then began to show me the ways He had been with me the entire time I was going through terrible things. I went and bought a Bible, which was the ONLY thing that kept me mentally stable enough to get through each day after I had finally kicked my prescription drug habit. In every situation I dealt with, I can now look back in that same Bible and find all the notes and page markers I used back then. Although I hadn't recommitted my life, God was still talking to me and keeping me. I no longer thought I was hearing voices or going crazy as my doctors had previously thought.

I was still in a very abusive relationship, a relationship that seemed to get worse when my ex-boyfriend found out I was studying God's word, trying to change, and trying to get away from him. I never understood why he was so livid about me reading my Bible. When I met him at college during my senior year, he had said he was a Christian. That is what initially attracted me to him. He was smart, a college student and went to church. I thought I'd hit the jackpot! But reality didn't play out that way.

I began praying regularly, and I wanted to be pleasing to God so badly. But my situation—living with my ex-boyfriend and having no job, no car, no money, no family to lean on, and no church home—kept me convinced that I was trying to do the impossible. I kept praying and kept believing God that if I would just take a small step, He would save me from the nightmare my life had become.

I found Victory World Church a year-and-a-half after I had bought my Bible. This church was different and to my surprise when I entered the church doors, I didn't burst into flames! Instead I was welcomed with open arms. The sanctuary is large and seats 1,500 people. I sat in the last seat making sure that I was not bringing attention to myself.

The message was amazing! I felt as though the Pastor was speaking directly to me. He led the sanctuary in a prayer of salvation and asked for all those who said the prayer and dedicated their lives to the Lord to raise their hands. I raised my hand because I was very proud of this momentous moment. The Pastor continued by asking everyone who had raised their hand to come down to the altar. I quickly put my hand down and stood there—not moving an inch. The woman next to me, who was a complete stranger, kindly offered to walk me to the altar. I snatched my hand back and politely said, *"no thank you"*. The lady continued to insist until I finally agreed and proceeded to the altar where God began to work on my shame, guilt and sheer disgust I had felt deep within my heart and soul.

After I left the altar, I had an immediate desire to change my life and circumstances. I left my boyfriend, got a new job, a cheap little affordable apartment, a nice little car, and even began talking to my family again.

I had never had more than one female friend, but I knew I didn't want to repeat my prior mistakes and allow wrong behaviors to take over like they had when I had the mentality of a man. I really needed women in my life—Godly women. I had only one female friend because I didn't trust women and thought they were gossipy and self-centered. Now I needed friends, family, someone to call in the midnight hour when my flesh rebelled against my spirit and it was all I could do to say, *"God please help me!"*

And help me... He did! I started attending a singles and young married couples group called "Fusion". I joined the group so I would have someone to talk too ... to have a friend ... to understand more of God and what He was all about. In that community, I was able to share my testimony—the nitty-gritty, down-and-dirty parts I had never even spoken out loud before. I was able to continue healing, growing, learning, and loving. I was shedding the old me, and I had amazing women right there beside me in the battle who are still my friends today. I was no longer just a shadow; I was becoming who God had intended me to be—a beautiful, pure woman.

At the start of this journey, I thought that God would never want me because of all the horrible things I'd done to myself, to other people, and to God Himself. God changed me! My family did not even recognize me, and sometimes they are still astonished at the change that's happened in my life...a change that began four years ago.

Yes, I have been set free! I can say that God kept me. Had it not been for Him, I could have been dead in a ditch and my family would never have known where I was. God redeemed and has restored me so I could share my struggles and encourage other women not to give up!

Regardless of the things you've done, even up to this very second, God still loves you. No matter what, He's still standing there with wide open arms waiting for you.

So many times, we keep ourselves away from God because we don't think He wants us. I was garbage; I was absolute trash. He has thrown away my dirty past—all my guilt and shame, my lonesomeness, and my searching—and He's made me into something new and better than I ever could ever have imagined. What the devil was trying his hardest to kill me with, God flipped over on him!

I have been happily married since October, 2005 to an amazingly gifted and anointed man who daily calls me his bride. We had a beautiful baby girl in November, 2008, and we are both involved in ministry. Not being in control of my life, and allowing God to take 100% control has freed my mind, my spirit, and my body. God truly has replaced the shame and filth of my past with a crown of jewels.

What have I learned the most from this journey is it's never too late, and nothing is too much for God to forgive. I now minister to women. ... ME? YES...ME! The masturbating, alcoholic, porn subscribing, sex addicted, prescription drug bingeing, sexually assaulted, voodoo bamboozled person I was, but now forever changed by the blood of Jesus.

I will never skimp on telling my story or the details of my past, because without them I wouldn't be Dede. I am Dede because of who I am... not who I want to be, or who I think I am ... but because of how God fashioned me and brought me through so very much.

Trials and Struggles to Joy and Victory

By Austin

I grew up going to church but never understood or saw it modeled before me that Christ wants a relationship with me, that He loves me and wants me to love and trust Him. We said prayers before dinner and bed but that was it. My Mom had some unresolved issues from growing up as a child of an alcoholic father, so she was an absentee Mom to say the least. Her years of repressed emotions turned to anger and rage that often times led to complete emotional breakdowns. She would scream and throw things, then lock herself in her room for days.

Early on I tried to please her and not rock the boat. I would tip toe around the house trying to keep her from erupting into a fit of rage. By the time I was 7 years old, a pattern had started to emerge. I would get home from school, and she would disappear to her room leaving me starring at the television. I would sneak to the kitchen to eat because it helped numb my pain, thus beginning my unhealthy relationship with food.

When my Dad got home at night from work it was like a beacon of hope. We spent a lot of time together in the evenings and on the weekends. He was doing double duty trying to make up for the fact that my Mom wasn't able to be there. I was wondering all the time what was wrong with Mom? Why didn't she want to be with me?

This cycle went on for years. It's what started me down a path of constantly looking to people and food to fill my emptiness. I had not been able to rely on my Mom, so I started putting all my hope in other people, people that are fallible.

I chose friends that were dominating and had the same traits my Mom had. I was always longing for unconditional love. Finally at 13 the quiet little girl who was trying to keep the peace had had enough. I started rebelling... quietly at first, but then giving up on friends, family and eventually God.

I was briefly involved in Youth Group at church. We would have different service projects and retreats that were teaching us what it looked like to be a Christ like servant. How to look outside of yourself to help others in need, or show love for someone you have never met by fixing up their house that was falling apart. I saw the same kind of service that Christ demonstrated when he washed the feet of the disciples as it talks about in John 13:5.

It was all happening right in front of me, but it was too late. I was more interested in what boy in the Youth Group could make me feel worthy. I was pushing God out and trying to fill the emptiness through boyfriends. That was just the beginning of a vicious cycle.

For the next 21 years it escalated from food and relationships to alcohol and drugs. At the age of 25, I ended up with a full-blown eating disorder, in an unhealthy relationship, pregnant and addicted to Methamphetamine. I became a person I never thought I could be. I was dying physically, spiritually and emotionally.

On the outside I was emaciated but finally skinny, so I thought this was good. On the inside I felt I had no soul, just an empty abyss. I had isolated myself from my family and my friends and was now failing out of school; everything was tumbling down around me. I could not go on another day living this miserable life. I could not take care of myself let alone make a friend, be a friend or lead a friend to Christ. God had another road for me to experience first.

After a sleepless night, I did not know where else to turn so I cried out to the God who I hadn't acknowledged in years. I was ready to do whatever He directed me to do.

The next day I told my therapist the whole truth. She was shocked to say the least. I had been hiding my meth addiction from her for two years and now I am pregnant. She knew my problem was bigger than both of us, so she suggested I go to inpatient rehab in Arizona.

I completely agreed, and was starting to feel the weight of the world lifted off my shoulders... Well, almost.

I was completely conflicted about being pregnant. How could this be a healthy pregnancy? I rarely ate and had been doing Meth every day for the past 6 months. I was in a terrible relationship and quite frankly, just a mess. I felt scared and alone so I took the easy way out and I had an abortion.

I tried to justify the abortion, but the feelings were overwhelming. How could a 25 year old be so irresponsible? Friends my age were trying to start families of their own and I had just disregarded this precious life that God had given me.

I medicated myself with drugs and alcohol every day for the next 3 weeks just to stay numb until I left for rehab.

Once I got there I had an opportunity to deal with all kinds of things, including the grief of having the last of four abortions. I think I only scratched the surface though. I went to an aftercare program for three more months then came home only to realize that a lifelong addiction would not go away over night.

I still had so much guilt, shame and unresolved feelings that without working a program I eventually drank again, which of course led to drugs and another bad relationship.

I was still trying to fill my God shaped hole with everything except God. This went on for two more years until literally God snatched me up out of the muck and mire (again) and placed me in a room full of recovering alcoholics.

Psalms 40:2 (NIV): *"He lifted me out of the slimy pit, out of the mud and mire; He set my feet on a rock and gave me a firm place to stand."*

He did just that! These people were happy and living the life I wanted to live. They embraced me whole heartedly, and were living what it talks about in John 15:15 (NIV): *"I no longer call you servants, because a servant does not know his master's business. Instead, I have called you friends, for everything that I had learned from my Father I have made known to you."*

As time went by, these women showed me the true definition of "make a friend, be a friend and bring a friend to Christ". That is the most basic definition of evangelism. These women modeled for me an authentic and God inspired way of what it means to be Christ like.

Through my pain and struggles and then victories, I can relate to someone else's pain and struggles to help them get back to Christ. There was nothing phony about Jesus, and there should be nothing phony about us. It's outlined very clearly in our program of recovery "tell your experience, strength and hope". Jesus prayed to the Father for wisdom and guidance: we should do the same.

I learned that the basis of my recovery depended on turning my life and will over to the care of God, as I understood Him. I knew it would be important to have a better understanding of who HE was, so I went back to church. Finally I found more people with the common goal of knowing Christ and making Christ known.

I have learned to carry His message into all aspects of my life in a very unique way because I understand alcoholism and am determined to minister to others in a loving, caring and respectful way.

When I discovered all the incredible revelations of who God was and how He was using my mess to minister to others, I was so excited that I immediately called my parents trying to tell them all the miraculous life changing things that had taken place in me. When I didn't get the overwhelming response I had hoped for, I felt disappointed. However, they told me they were excited that I had found peace and fulfillment. St. Frances said, "Preach the Gospel daily and if necessary... use words.

Christ has not given up on anyone and neither will I. I have a tendency to burn bridges with people. If they are not doing something the way I think they should or in the timeframe that fits my expectations, I get frustrated and pull away. I am constantly reminded of the fact that I had a lot of people praying for me when I was such a mess and they did not give up on me.

This same principal also applies to forgiveness. I am reminded daily that it is only because of God's grace and forgiveness that I have any of the miraculous things in my life that I do today.

My parents and I have continued emotional healing from the past, and my Mom and I are walking out our Christian journey together. I have been blessed with a wonderful caring and loving Husband that is completely supportive of my life in recovery and the best miracle of all, a 16-month-old precious little boy that I love with all my heart.

Based on my past mistakes I thought I would not be able to have children, but I was limiting the scope of God's forgiveness with my human mind. HE knows no limits.

I now share my story to give God the glory by working with other alcoholic women. That means guiding and encouraging each of them in their spiritual growth. I had a loving sponsor do that for me, so now I must do the same for someone else. Her action led to my action.

It is my joy to take the light Jesus has shined into my life, and shine it into other's lives. I have been taught that Christ has not just saved us FROM something, but saved us TO something. We come to know God the Father and Jesus through the loving acts of others.

The Modern Day Woman at the Well

By Dawn Adcox

"If abortion had been legal, you'd have never been born!" And how about living ten miles from your own daughter but never calling or asking to see her? Do you think those things might have an impact on a young person's self-worth? I can tell you from experience those words and actions hurt. The old cliché, "sticks and stones may break my bones but words will never hurt me," does NOT hold true when it involves loved ones speaking to one another, especially if the one speaking is a parent talking to a child. That is where my story begins.

Did my mom love me when she spoke those harsh words to me? Does she love me now? I can emphatically say, "Yes, my mom loves me." Can I also say that when she was young she was angry and full of her own hurt? Yes, I can say that, too! Was my mom showing extremely bad judgment when she opened her mouth and spoke such words to me? Yes, I can say she was.

What about my biological father? Did he love me? I reckon in his own way he did. I guess he figured if I needed him, I would call. Little did he know that by not showing any interest—by not wanting to see me or spend time with me—it caused me to wonder for years why I wasn't good enough.

I am a modern day Samaritan woman—a woman very similar to the one written about in the Bible in the Book of John, Chapter Four. The story begins with a woman who goes all alone in the early afternoon to fetch water from a well. Jesus, who is at that well with no jar or bucket, asks her for a drink of water. During their conversation, Jesus tells her to go get her husband and come back. This is where she and I come together. The woman told Jesus she did not have a husband, and He answered, "You are right. You have had five husbands and are now living with another man." You got it! She'd had five husbands! She was at the well to draw water when no one else was around because she was an outcast. Having multiple husbands at that point in history was not socially acceptable.

Now her story and my story don't exactly line up, but I have been married four times. I have two children, each with a different last name, and neither of their last names match my current last name. Before I continue with my story, let me ask you this question: Is it socially acceptable today for a woman to have multiple marriages and children by different husbands? No, it is not.

Many times I wanted to bow my head in shame when someone asked me where my daughter's or son's dad lived or had to explain my children's age difference and how long my current husband and I have been married.

My mistakes and bad judgment were weighing me down. How can you make new friends and invite them into your life when you believe everyone is looking at you with judging eyes?

The natural question for you to ask is, "Were you saved when all of this was going on?" I mean, surely a woman covered by the blood of Jesus would not be married that many times or carry that much guilt. Fortunately, even though my mom and my step-dad never went to church or took my little brother and me to church, they didn't keep me from getting onto the Baptist bus that came by on Sunday mornings.

As a twelve year old, I walked, all alone, down that l-o-o-o-o-o-ng church aisle and answered the call of the Holy Spirit. I really didn't know what I was doing, and when that nice man—probably a Deacon—asked me if I was a Christian, I said, "No, I'm a Methodist!" Thankfully, he rephrased the question and asked if I had Jesus in my heart? I said "YES" and was baptized a few weeks later. Even though I didn't really know what it meant to be a Christian, I was attuned to the prompting of the Holy Spirit.

I would love to report that my steps of faith at that church took me safely through adolescence, but it didn't. The hole in my heart needed human affection and affirmation. The absence of felt love left a deep emptiness that my brief relationship with God did not sustain. It was hard to appropriate the love of the Father with no spiritual encouragement at home. Although Mom supported me in other areas of my life, there was no affection and no positive response to my accomplishments. She guided us by negatives and criticism. This was the enemy's opportunity to convince me of my worthlessness and failure. Looking back through adult eyes I can see that my family members really did care deeply about me. They demanded obedience to rules as expression of their love — yet my heart was desperate for validation as a person.

I did have the advantage of being smart, tall, pretty and athletic. That was plenty enough to keep boys in my life full time. With my longing for love and affection, sex was only a small step away. It felt good. It was a way to be "close," momentarily filling that life-long need inside me for intimacy. I was quick to say "I love you" then off to the next partner with another "I love you." I didn't think about the baggage I was piling on myself that would eventually weigh me down to destructive levels.

I seldom made it to church and didn't really derive much immediate encouragement there. Yet God used that time to remind me that He was there and He loved me. Even though that truth slipped in and out of my mind, it would prove a firm foundation down the road.

Following college I moved to a small town with a new job. Part of my new start was to begin attending church again. Because of my failure to make a solid connection with my new church family and my lack of biblical knowledge I was soon discouraged. But I was not discouraged with meeting new guys and began racking up more sexual partners. One of these men was extremely nice and soon my friends were urging me to consider marriage. Even though we announced love for one another, our differences were enormous. While I agreed to a wedding, my heart told me this was a mistake. Twelve months and one affair later we divorced. Guilt and shame once again filled my broken heart.

Then along came husband number two. He was Sauvé and debonair—quite the womanizer, actually—and I fell for it hook, line, and sinker. He told me why he and his first wife had gotten a divorce and his indiscretion ... but I didn't tell him about mine. I thought, "Wow, if he had an affair, then that is what I deserve. We have a lot in common." So, we got married.

My new husband had two precious children from his previous marriage who were five and eight years old, and we had a daughter of our own (my pride and joy).

I had been attending church all this time. Now my new husband came with me and we both became very involved: Sunday school, mission trips, choir and discipleship classes. I was growing and learning but I was still so needy and was difficult to live with.

My husband eventually found his secretary to be more appealing than I was and had no problem parading her around. When I finally had enough, we divorced. I couldn't make a clean break that time because we had a daughter. That didn't stop me, however, from quickly swinging into another unhealthy relationship.

Eventually the company I worked for relocated me to another state. The heartbreak here was that my daughter's joint custody arrangement kept her away from me for lengthy periods of time. My solid trust in God's power carried me through.

I found a good church immediately and God put three mentors into my life who encouraged serious spiritual growth in so many areas of daily living — but it failed to reach all of my fleshly personal habits. I spent hours walking and running while praying for God's forgiveness and total cleaning of my life. I was still hurting, but for the first time I felt free and clean. This took me closer to my Father than I had ever experienced. In spite of vowing to become sexually pure, another poor decision and more trouble was close by.

With my daughter far away and time on my hands, my godly friends were not able to protect me from my "old self" indiscretions. Almost seamlessly I had returned to the bar/party scene, where I met the next significant man in my life. He wanted to have sex of course — and so we did. When I was at church I was that other person, who wanted to live right and when I came home I would tell my boyfriend that sex outside of marriage was out! His disapproval of my church life was understandable. So I quit hanging out with my Christian friends and began spending full time with his friends.

All this time the Holy Spirit was screaming to me, "Get away from him; do not marry him. LISTEN TO ME!" I heard but did not listen. I was like Paul in Roman 7:15: *"I do not understand what I do. For what I want to do I do not do, but what I hate, I do."* So I married again.

Our marriage was miserable. I found myself with the same old degrading, belittling behavior directed toward me. We had a big house but no friends. We hung out with his parents, who lived next door. I got pregnant immediately, and I gave birth to a wonderful little boy. At that time I gained full custody of my daughter, so now we were a family of four.

In spite of family church attendance, I soon realized this husband was not meeting my needs — needs that only God could fill. A new friend came into the picture and he was a fresh face amidst the boredom of an unfulfilled marriage relationship. Trouble came head-on and I filed for divorce. Because of my emotional and physical connection with my new relationship I lost custody of my son. I was shattered and broken. Added to that defeat, my Pastor asked me to step away from the various church activities in which I had taken leadership. In my abandoned state I felt miles away from God.

I needed a friend, and to my surprise that friend was my mom! She moved close to me to be of help. A huge healing time started to take place inside of me and it began with the relationship between me and my mom. I was also struggling through another failed marriage. It was time to take stock and decide who I really wanted to be. That man to whom I turned in my need of true relationship became my fourth husband. Although we had been living in sin, God was at work in both of us. He, a Pastor's son and me, a broken, wounded sinner, together were redeemed in a final, resolute manner.

Shortly after our marriage we answered the Holy Spirit's call and walked down the aisle together — this time to state publicly our commitment to trust and obey our Lord as a family. Since that time, my two children have answered the Savior's call and have been baptized and my Pastor asked me to share the story of my life. I bared my soul, and using the woman at the well in John 4 as an illustration, I revealed my past brokenness and my present victories.

God's word is true. Romans 8:1-2 says, *"...there is now no condemnation for those who are in Christ Jesus, because through Christ Jesus the law of the Spirit of life sets me free from the law of sin and death."* I am redeemed, and the enemy has no power over me! I am free from the baggage that the enemy wants me to carry! I have laid it at the cross, and today and every day I cast my burdens upon the Lord and He sustains me. (Psalm 55:22)

Like the Samaritan woman at the well, I have left my jar (my burden) at the well and am telling everyone what my Lord has done for me ... for He knows everything I have ever done and will ever do, and He still loves me and forgives me. Praise God!

"Then leaving her water jar, the woman went back to the town and said to the people, 'Come see a man who told me everything I ever did'" (John 4:28-29 NIV).

God of Peace and Understanding

By Trisha Petty

"All things work together for the good, to those who know and love God and are called and ordained to his purpose" (Romans 8:28 KJV). We rattle that scripture off with such hopeful abandon, and as I faced the 'junk' in my life, that verse worked very well; helping me keep my head up high with my eyes on Jesus as I plowed through.

That was *until* my wedding night, when my handsome bridegroom came out of the bathroom all strong, young, and powerful. I shrieked in terror and ended up on the 5th floor hotel balcony trying to jump to get away from him. We laugh about it now, but at that time, he was so scared he called the paramedics to give me a shot to calm me down.

In the following weeks and months, we began to understand that in my childhood I had been sexually abused. It took several years of therapy with psychiatrists and counselors—some of them godly men and women and some of them not so godly—to help me work out all of my emotional and physical issues concerning the rapes I endured as a young girl.

We had some troubles consummating our wedding vows because every time my husband would come near me, I would go into hysterics. He used 'non-verbal non-sexual touching' to woo me all over. We married in December, by March he had gained my trust and I was ready and immediately became pregnant. During my physical examination due to my pregnancy is when the doctor discovered evidence that I had been sexually abused. The damage inside me was so extensive that the doctor didn't think I would carry to term. My husband made the decision that we would carry the baby, *"as the Lord opens the womb and closes the womb"*.

But now we knew why I was so upset when my young husband came near me. I read a lot during the pregnancy, worked on my Doctorate and Masters degrees as I was bed ridden through three months to the day I finally broke my water. The Lord gave us a beautiful baby girl, born by C-section and presently is a happy mother of two.

However, it took several years of therapy with psychiatrists and counselors to work out all my inner emotional and physical issues about the rape.

With my first appointment I was tested and diagnosed to be Bi-Polar (Manic Depressive) so we added the medication to keep that in check.

I had a therapist who helped me find creative ways to build my self image while loving my husband without getting into the physical part of our relationship. I had lots of great ideas given to me and one of the best was to pray over my husband while doing his laundry. While I was putting the laundry away I would specifically pray over my husband by praying over his work pants and shirts. I would pray over his work, his co-workers, even the weather that could affect his work. Also while ironing his shirts that he wore to church and school, I would pray for his Pastor, his Sunday School class, his teachers and classmates. Thirty years later I still do this but with a twist. As I hang up my own clothes, I pray for the people I touch at my job or church when I wear that outfit. That small piece of advice changed my simple prayer life to a powerful prayer life. To this day my husband tells me I am the prayer warrior that gets things done, but only if there is a lot of laundry!

One of the bad pieces of advice was from a therapist who suggested that I have an affair. His summation was that we were 'doing it' wrong and that if I had an affair that would teach me something new, so I could teach my husband.

After receiving such bad advice, I was invited by a client to 'drop by his hotel'. He was very – very attractive and I had many hours of access to him. How easily I could have gone out and broken my vows and no one would have known. With a friendly smile I was able to look him straight in the eye and say with pride, "I can't do that...I am bad at it!"

The advice of this therapist proved to be so anti-Bible, anti-marriage that of course I dismissed his suggestion and fired him. I learned much about the power I had of getting good doctors and therapists to work with me and for me. To understand what medications I was taking and their effects, I was always careful to listen to which advice I would heed. Even Christian Counselor's can dispense bad advice, but for me, it was the minor session with my Pastor that changed the pivotal course of my life.

I was working hard with my healing, forgiving and moving on... but I was still steeped into the *"why me"* syndrome of it all. I was working it all out but not on my own. I had my anchors with Jesus on my right hand, my therapists on my left, and my husband covering my back and loving me the best he could. I was growing and healing... but I was still stuck in the *"why me"* syndrome. Then my Pastor asked me, *"Why NOT you?"*

I have always been amazed at how God uses the little things in my life. For me, it's those little words: if, and, but, or, and in this case, <u>NOT</u>.

Pastor Curtis brought out Romans 8:28 again to me, and asked me to read it. After I read, *"All things work together for the good, to those who know and love God and called according to his purpose,"* he asked, *"Do you see the condition?"*

I had never thought about a *'condition.'* I had always focused on the first part, *"all things work for the good."*

Pastor pointed out, "called according to His purpose." He asked, *"Do you think there was a purpose to all of this?"*

I remember being flippant, almost cavalier, with my answer: *"The purpose was so I will rely on Him more and not look to men for answers."*

Pastor Curtis shook his head. *"Try again,"* he said.

"The bad stuff shows the world when I rely on God how much God loves me and that He can love them?"

Pastor shook his head once more.

I looked at him like a deer caught in the headlights of a Ford pickup truck. I hate it when I don't know the answers.

Then Pastor Curtis said something so profound that it changed my life. "*You stand at a crossroad, Trisha*," he said.

"*You stand with two choices in front of you. You can take the path of knowing that you have found a Daddy in Heaven who loves you very much and go comfortably on with your little mediocre existence, or you can use this dreadful, awful thing that happened to you to help others. You can _earn_ the gifts of empathy, compassion, a listening ear, arms eager to hug, and shoulders to cry on, or you can go on your safe, comfortable way, facing life with no personal understanding of forgiveness and acceptance ... because you have done neither so far in your life with this situation. I encourage you to find a way to use this horrible thing for the betterment of the gospel, of your fellow believers, and of yourself ... and heaven will rejoice at the victory over the enemy.*"

Since I had already been writing short stories and working on a novel for some time, I heeded Pastor Curtis' insight and wrote several books based on my rape and Bi-polar condition. Through other women's stories, I completed 15 novels dealing with crimes against women and children. The writing gave me a relief of my burden and opened opportunities for me to speak in class rooms and at writer's conferences, conventions and other places that would normally never have allowed a follower of Christ to speak. I was able to speak with understanding and compassion on a whole other level about depression, loneliness, fear, anger, hate, peace, fulfillment, strength, forgiveness, and love.

What exactly made me think that I was all that special to be immune to ever having bad stuff happen in my life? I am not immune to sin; I am not immune to stupidity; I am not immune to disobedience. What made me think that I am so incredibly special that I shouldn't have had to face a rape, the death of a loved one, a divorce, the death of a child, or other life changing issues? Even God's own Son had to face bad stuff in his life. Facing the cross was no easy matter for Jesus. I am no more special than other Christians who face those things. I am a daughter of the King, to be sure, but even princesses have problems.

I do, however, have a heavenly King—a Father who has been beside me through it all and continues to be there for me every day. He is faithfully holding my hand, holding my arm, even holding my entire body when I need it. He alone can calm my mind, my heart, and my spirit with His words, with His Spirit, and with His pure presence.

When I can't sleep at night for the Enemy comes to bring back smells, fears, tastes, sounds of those nights I was tortured, Jesus reminds me of a happy place we have. One of the therapists had me tell her of the most beautiful place I had ever seen. After describing it to her, she told me to put Jesus there. Now when I am being tormented in my memories, I go to my special place, find my Jesus waiting there, take some deep cleansing breaths and 'come home' to Jesus. He calms me, comforts me and soon I am asleep.

My father had deeply hurt me by raping me at the age of nine months to five years of age. He had deserted me through the divorce of my mother and brought me to the brink of suicide by the age of thirty. My Heavenly Father has never brought me harm, has never left me, and is never far from me. He always encourages, lifts, and soothes my spirit.

It is with many tears and with anguish and understanding that I can stand and read Paul's words in Philippians 4:4-9 (NKJV): "*Rejoice in the Lord always. Again I will say, rejoice! Let your gentleness be known to all men. The Lord is at hand. Be anxious for nothing, but in everything by prayer and supplication, with thanksgiving, let your requests be made known to God; and the peace of God, which surpasses all understanding, will guard your hearts and minds through Christ Jesus. Finally, brethren, whatever things are true, whatever things are noble, whatever things are just, whatever things are pure, whatever things are lovely, whatever things are of good report, if there is any virtue and if there is anything praiseworthy — meditate on these things. The things which you learned and received and heard and saw in me, these do, and the God of peace will be with you.*"

And you know what? The God of peace has truly been with me!

A Dead Cow, a Tidal Wave, and Deliverance

By Teasi Cannon

What should you get when you throw a very small pebble into a quiet pond? Small ripples, that's what. Well, one day that small pebble caused a tidal wave in my life. Looking back, I can see what God was up to, but at the time... let's just say I was a mess.

The day was beautiful. It was sunny and warm – a perfect Saturday. The occasion: a baby shower. Around 50 women from my church had gathered to lavish a young expectant mother with gifts and share words of blessing and advice. The food was great. The fellowship, sweet. All was going well until "the pebble" arrived.

The pebble: The mother of the expectant mother (say that ten times fast) called for a time of prayer. This is something the women of my church almost always do: praying for the delivery, the baby, and the new family life to come, etc. Since the group was so large, the "mother of the mother" hand-picked a few women to come forward. One by one she invited each elder's wife in attendance. She invited them all...but me.

Enter tidal wave. I couldn't believe what was happening. *How can she leave me out? I am an elder's wife! Why would she do that? What is wrong with me?* Feelings of rejection rose in me faster than – well, pretty darn fast. I felt like I was going to throw up. A cold chill ran up and down my spine while hot tears sprang to my eyes. I thought I was going to lose it completely.

Lucky for me every head was bowed and every eye was closed. The praying had begun. I sank as far back into a corner as I could and took several deep breaths to keep myself from whelping like a wounded cat. Tears kept trying to claw their way out of my eyes, as I dove deep within the recesses of my mind for some sort of salvation – perhaps a thought that would distract me, helping me to make it through these prayers with some composure. I needed something really good. Maybe something funny.

What I landed on was kind of funny, but mostly gross.

I realize this may seem disturbing, but what I chose to meditate on while a sweet and holy moment was occurring on the other side of the room was...my dog sniffing a dead cow's rear quarters. Now, before you judge me, I didn't create this thought. This is a scene which happened earlier that very morning right outside my kitchen window. Living on a farm, scenes such as this were quite common. I couldn't help it that this particular memory happened to come into my mind at just the perfect time. It did its job, though.

As soon as the last "amen" was said, I put on the best fake smile and hugged those who were standing along my path to the door. I told the last woman I saw that I was "so sorry" I had to leave early, but that I had somewhere else to be. I nearly sprinted to my van, started it up and peeled out of the gravel driveway – tires spitting rocks at the family dog. Tears finally broke through the barricade I had put up, and rushed down my face in rivers. I drove away from those women I had known for years - mentally shooting each and every one of them the bird (I know...I was bad).

Home at last, I threw open my front door – startling my sweet husband who gave me the "What on earth happened to you?" look – and ran quickly to my bedroom. I threw my purse on the floor, and I threw myself on the bed. Face down. Legs and arms sprawled out. And I cried. And I cried. And then I cried some more.

Then I let Him have it – God, that is. *What is wrong with me? Why don't people like me? Why do I get hurt everywhere I go? Why did you make me this way? Why? Why?*

When He could slip in a few words of His own, this is what I heard: "Do you really want to know?"

Of course I want to know. I can't live like this anymore!

"Okay, then. Get quiet a minute and take my hand. I'm going to show you something."

Into my mind came a memory from my childhood. I was seven or eight years old at the time. I was visiting my aunt in Florida, and even though I didn't want to stay without my mom, she left me there to play with my cousins. Not long after mom left, my aunt left for work. We kids were then in the care of my uncle.

"Time to play a game, kiddos. You know the one." Oh, I knew the one, alright. I'd played it before – a type of hide-and-seek. Only we didn't hide. Our underwear did. Uncle watched as we slid off our panties, and then he'd go hide them. If we found them, we won and got to pick the next activity. If we lost – well, he got to pick. And he always won.

He won that day, too, and the next thing I knew my little naked body was pushed to the floor, hands bound, rag shoved in my mouth, and innocence taken as tears streaked my little girl cheeks.

Oh, God, not this memory again.

"Yes. Keep watching."

But how could you let that happen to me? Wasn't I cute enough? Wasn't I sweet enough? Didn't my life matter at all?

"Keep watching."

A new character entered my memory – one I never remembered seeing before. He was ugly. He was dark. He walked up to my little body, knelt down on the floor so he could speak right into my ear, and he said, "You are trash, little girl. No one loves you. Your life isn't even worth protecting. Even your mom left you here." Then he looked right into my eyes, smiled a grin that was pure evil, stood and walked away.

Back on my bed more tears erupted. *That was the devil, wasn't it? The devil was there?*

"That's right, sweet girl. He spoke lies right into your very soul that day – lies you've believed ever since."

I have, haven't I? As a little girl, when I felt so much rejection, I was believing the lie?

"Yes."

As a teenager, when I was desperate for boys to like me no matter what it took, I was believing the lie?

"Yes."

Every Sunday I left church wounded because I wasn't included in this meeting or that – I was believing the lie?

"Yes. You believed the lies. Now, let me show you one more thing."

Back in the room where my little body lay, another new figure sat in the corner of the room. It was a man, sitting on the floor with his arms wrapped tightly around his knees. He was rocking back and forth in agony, tears streaming down his face as he looked with deep love into my eyes.

It is Jesus, isn't it?

"Yes. It is my Son."

Why didn't He get up and protect me?

"He did. He protected you on the Cross. He saved the deepest part of you – the part that can never die. He protected the part of you that responds to my voice. His heart bled for you – my heart bleeds for you. You are my beloved. Your life matters to me."

I sat on my bed for quite some time longer that day, letting the truth I'd just experienced find its way into the broken places of my heart. God works in supernatural ways, and it is nearly impossible to describe exactly how healing occurred that day. But it did. Chains fell off me as I came to realize that the Father of Lies had stolen far too much from me.

Now I know – without any doubt – that my life matters. I know that I am loved, not only by my Heavenly Father, but by my friends and family. I know I am adored. I am the daughter of the King, and the devil can't have me.

And whenever he tries again to whisper lies into my ears, I tell him to speak to the hand – the hand of my Heavenly Daddy. That shuts him right up.

"For I will restore health to you and heal you of your wounds," says the Lord. (Jeremiah 30:17)

Not long after this encounter with healing, God enabled me to forgive the man who had taken so much from me. I can honestly say that when I think of my uncle today, I harbor no resentment, no bitterness, no desire for revenge. But I couldn't have done it without a special gift from Above.

The gift? A perspective greater than my own.

Although I don't know for sure what kind of childhood my uncle had, I have no doubt he was wounded. God showed me a bit of His take on the man: He gave me a vision of my uncle as a little boy – a boy being molested himself. No details were necessary, only the realization that somewhere along the line, my uncle was lied to, as well. Sometime in his little boy life – a time when his heart was vulnerable and raw – the devil whispered a lie into his soul. Perhaps the lie was that no one would ever want him. Perhaps the lie was that he would never be normal. I'm not sure, but I know he believed it. His actions with children prove he believed it.

So, although what he did to me will never, never be okay; I have been able to take my uncle off my "hook" and put him on God's. He is a criminal. He is a pervert. But he is also a very wounded man.

I trust that my Heavenly Father loves me more than I can ever understand, and He is not okay with the wrongs that were done to me – not one bit! However, I also believe that His vengeance is pure. Mine isn't. I would have severed a body part - if you know what I mean – but that would accomplish nothing.

My forgiveness didn't benefit my uncle, but it did take a huge burden off of me. It's not my concern anymore; it's God's. I have officially dropped my uncle off at the foot of Jesus's Cross, wiped my hands of the matter; and moved on into the freedom, hope, and inheritance befitting a princess like me.

It's Only a Book!

By Betty Clot

The earliest memory I have while searching my past is hiding in the linen closet for what seemed like hours at a time because I was so afraid. I remember being awake while everyone else was asleep because of my fear.

I also remember things that were good like my grandmother whom I loved that lived down the street from us and several good friends I had whom I played with. My father's parents lived in a rural community and were very stern and not very loving. I never enjoyed going to their house. In later years, my father told me that he never remembered my grandparents ever asking about his day, telling him they loved him, or ever giving any indication that he was loved and appreciated.

My father did not attend church, but two of his brothers became Christians and were very loving and kind. However, my memory of those gatherings was of the men gathered on the front porch, smoking, chewing and drinking.

My father became a working alcoholic and was a hard worker.

When he came home is when he did his drinking and became harsh and cruel. My father never hit my mother but their arguments were loud and scary. When they argued, I hid. When I got older I would just climb a tree and read a book.

We moved out of state when I was ten years old and that is when my addiction to reading began. We lived in a series of homes, sometimes moving three times a year, which meant three different schools. I was very shy, and it took me a while to make new friends. It seemed that every time I would make a friend, we would move again. This was a very difficult and painful time for me as a young girl and reading became my escape for many years to come.

Many years later, I met my precious husband at church but at first I didn't like him. We started dating and all we did was talk, talk, talk. Because we talked so much, he was the first person who truly knew my heart and soul. My husband was blessed to have a faithful Sunday School teacher who visited him and always showed him the love of Jesus while he was growing up. He also had a good friend who invited him to come to church. Because of the love they showed him, my husband had not only grown into a very Godly man, but he also became a preacher.

So now I am a preacher's wife. However, the addiction I had as a child for reading was still with me. I read incessantly. If I didn't have a book to read, I was frantic. I would go anywhere and do whatever it took to get a book. I didn't care what kind of book it was. I had to have a book! It was my drug of choice. It lifted me out of myself and transported me to a different plane. I neglected many things because I was reading. I read while cooking (burned quite a few meals), washing dishes, sweeping floors, you name it. I constantly had to have a book in my hand. It was so consuming that many nights I would read the entire night, and struggle to do what needed to be done the next day. I was totally out of control.

I finally came to myself and realized what a hold, an addiction I had to reading when we had gone to my husband's father's funeral. There was a huge snowstorm which covered the entire east coast and we could not get back home. We were stuck at our son's house for almost a week and I ran out of books! Horrors! I remembered seeing a used book store several blocks away. I got to the store and although I realized it was a pornography shop, I went in anyway and bought a used Harlequin Romance novel. You could just imagine the stares that I received from the men in the store. One of the men said, "*I never saw anything like this before.*" After satisfying my addiction and where it took me to have a book in my hand, I was so ashamed that

I prayed to God to deliver me from that problem. God heard my broken and contrite heart to free me and He did!

I still like to read, but I no longer HAVE to read. I no longer MUST read the entire book before I put it down. And I ONLY read Christian books. God gave me a miracle that day that I will cherish forever.

People chuckle with respect when I tell them I understand their addictions because of my past addiction to reading books. They think that reading cannot be as harmful as other addictions. I believe that any addiction, anything that we put above God (work, drugs, alcohol, reading, etc.) is a sin when you are consumed by it and it rules you. The question should always be what is the root of that addiction? What caused me to be so consumed with reading that I always wanted to escape from reality? Isn't that where addictions usually start?

God gave me another miracle thirty-five years ago. My husband was the Pastor of his first church and while there, I became seriously ill with gall bladder disease. The doctors couldn't figure out what was wrong. Test after test was run, but no one could figure out what the problem was. I was told it was all in my mind. I finally had an exploratory surgery where they discovered my gall bladder was so diseased that it could not absorb the dye used in the tests. The doctor told me I was a hairs breath from dying.

I was in the hospital a week with a roommate I could not stand. She was everything I was not. She was a barmaid, she drank, she cussed and I didn't like her. I didn't like her at all! We were both scheduled to be dismissed the same day. As we were lying in our beds in complete silence waiting for the doctor to come dismiss us, a voice came very strongly in my mind saying, *"Tell her I love her"*. The great Christian that I was, I said, *"NO, I don't like her!"* The voice came again saying, *"You must tell her I love her."* With a heart full of bitterness I said, *"Do you know God loves you?"* then turned towards her with a frown on my face to see her reaction.

She looked at me with pain and unbelief on her face and replied, *"No, I didn't!"* My heart broke! I saw that the great sinner in that room was NOT her, but ME! I knew better. She didn't. Praise God, she accepted the gift God offered.

I truly believe that my hospital visit was not about my sickness but about her salvation and about the condition of my heart. A lot of the feelings I had towards my roommate in the hospital resulted from the anger I had bottled up towards alcohol and how it affected my father and our relationship. I wanted nothing to do with *anything* alcoholic.

However, at that very moment God worked a miracle in my life of beginning to have a great love for those who are trapped in addictions. Yes, that experience birthed the beginning of a ministry dear to my heart that enables me to do the work I now do, founding and administrating a rehabilitation halfway house for those ladies who come out of jail and want to get help. God has certainly had His hand on my heart and on this ministry. All praise is due to Him!

I love God with all my heart and mind. I could not do the work He has given me without constant prayer, constantly being covered with the armor of God and daily asking for strength and wisdom. I am so grateful that He allows me to grow day by day. I know the day I stop growing will be the day I graduate from this life into His Heavenly home. I am so glad that He gives us chance after chance to grow and become more like Jesus. He never gives up on us!

Through it all, God who began a good work in us, IS going to bring it to completion if we just step out of the way and allow God to be God and allow the work to be done in our hearts. My part is to be continuously willing to grow, change and be transformed.

Betty Clot is the Founder of The Discipleship House located in Columbia, Tennessee. She and her husband Walter, have three married sons, seven grandchildren and one great grandchild.

For the Love of a Child

By Alicia Martin

I was born to be a victim—at least statistically speaking. I had an absentee, alcoholic father, a violent and abusive step-father, and a passive mother. I had no idea that this beginning pattern would follow me for a large part of my life.

I met the man in a bar and I knew better. I had left my husband after fourteen years because he had once again, cheated on me. I was sad, lonely, depressed, and my self-esteem was at rock bottom. When I saw this guy standing against the post at the club, I knew I would go home with him. He was the polar opposite of my husband: he had tattoos, earrings, and spiky hair. I was married to Mr. GQ, and I knew this guy was the opposite. That was appealing ... but I had no idea what was to come.

Within weeks, I had moved in with him. He was enthralled with me and I found that refreshing. I was pleased that someone showed such interest when I had received such distain from my husband, who had told me so many times, "If you hadn't gotten fat, I would not have had to cheat on you". This new guy made me feel beautiful. He could not stand to be away from me for even a moment. At the time, I didn't realize how dangerous that would become.

The first time he hurt me, I was shocked. We had been arguing, and I went to leave. His eyes turned stormy—I could see them change from blue to black—and I was deathly afraid. I ran from the house, but he caught me. He wrapped his hands around my throat and did not let go until I sank to the ground. Afterwards, he cried and told me he had never done that before. I believed him. As stupid as that may sound,

I believed him. And I believed that it would never happen again. But it did.

At the time I moved in with him, I was in a custody battle with my ex-husband. The courts frowned upon us "living together," so we got married. It made sense at the time, but the day I married him, he slapped me across the face and busted my lip. And it didn't stop there.

I could tell when it was coming. For weeks life would get worse and worse ... his moods becoming darker and darker. Then we would argue, and eventually it would happen again. I was almost relieved when he hit me or pushed me or strangled me because that meant a few weeks or months of peace. Afterwards, life was good for awhile. He was apologetic, remorseful, and almost sweet. But I always knew it would happen again.

I left him several times, but I always went back. I don't know why ... I just always went back. I believed his promises and apologies. The last time, I hadn't even been home for a day when it started. He told me that everything was my fault and I had no right to leave with his "boy."

My family had quit trying to help. They were too angry. They had helped again and again, only to watch me return again to live with the monster. Now I was on my own.

One day my daughter was walking the dog when the dog got away from her and was hit by a car. She was devastated, but his response was to yell at her and curse her on the phone. I called my ex-husband to pick my daughter up in order to save her from her step-dad's tirade. She called me the next day to tell me she would not be coming home.

I had lost my daughter who mattered more to me than life itself. It was more than I could bear and I overdosed and prayed for death. Then, I saw my beautiful son sleeping on the couch. I could not leave him with no one to protect him, so I ran to the bathroom and vomited while begging God to let me live.

At the hospital, my husband stayed by my side. Whenever the psychiatrist came in, he would not budge, so I did not speak of how things were. They discharged me with a prescription for anti-depressants, anti-anxiety medication, and sleeping pills along with a follow-up appointment with the doctor.

When I spoke to the doctor alone the next day, I told him what was happening. I asked him how long I would have to take medication and his reply was, "as long as you are with the son of a b—." Truer words were never spoken.

I existed on meds for two more years. I quit caring about the fights, the violence and myself. I just quit. Then, one day, the worst happened. My four-year old son came into the living room and shot his dad in the face with a tiny little Nerf toy gun. His dad snapped on him and grabbed our child by the throat and slammed him to the ground. I screamed, as did my son. I took my son in my arms and for a moment I saw myself killing his father. For a moment I saw the blood gush from his body as I stabbed him over and over and over. I cradled my baby in my arms and I prayed, "GOD, PLEASE HELP ME!"

I made plans. I was leaving and taking my children, and this time I would not return. He came home the evening before I was to go (he did not know, of course) and caught me on the phone. He grabbed my neck and told me, "*If I catch you, they'll never find your body. I will throw you in the wood chipper, and they will never find the pieces!*"

The following day, he went to work. I went to work and called him (so he would know I was at work). Then, I returned home and packed a few things. I went back to work and called him again ... then back to the house to pick up as much as I could fit into the car. I went back to work and called him one last time. I told him that I would be in the dining room for an hour and would call after I had finished serving lunch to the patients. I ran to my car, picked my children up from school/daycare, and drove. I drove for four days. I did not stop until I reached Arizona, where I immediately went into a domestic violence shelter with my children.

I had gotten away ... or so I thought. I found a job and got us a place to live. We had finally begun a new life far away from my husband.

My dear friend was the Director of the Maury County Center Against Domestic Violence. I kept in touch with her and she relayed payments for my car and watched the papers for me. It finally appeared—an ad searching for me to file for divorce. I had thirty days to respond or my husband would be granted the divorce and sole custody of my son. I had a choice, and I chose to return and fight.

I wish I could say "the good guys won, and we all lived happily ever after." Wouldn't that be nice? But it was not so. I was reprimanded for running away, and the court battle began. The court appointed a guardian ad litem for my son. She did not believe that I had been abused, and recommended that the father receive primary custody. Eventually, we settled out of court for shared custody.

Two years later, the battle still rages. We are now in another custody battle. My son is being torn apart by a violent father, and I will not stop until justice is served. I have found my voice and have quit hiding in the corner with my hands over my head. *I speak to protect my son. I speak to protect others who are living in a silent hell. **I speak for myself and all that I have lost. And I thank the Lord every day for granting me the strength to continue fighting.***

I remember running down the street one day as my husband chased me. It was rush hour, and we lived on the main street. As he grabbed me by the hair and started dragging me back into the house, I remember watching as car after car passed. No one stopped. No one called the police as he took me inside and brutalized me. I remember how helpless I felt, how I thought no one cared about me, and how I prayed that there would be a knock on the door and help would arrive. I will never again be silent about this plague which is domestic violence. I will not "drive past" and pretend I do not see.

Today, life is different. It is still difficult, and I still have many struggles ahead concerning my son and his father. But today is brighter. I am brighter. The darkness that so engulfed me has lifted, and there is such a glorious break in the clouds.

I have spent many sleepless nights watching my child suffer through night terrors and rage problems. I questioned God for years and asked, *"Why me?"* I now thank Him daily and I know why – another mother may have hurt this special child. Another mother may have given up. Another mother may have walked away. The Lord trusted me with this child and I am eternally grateful for that trust.

I have completed my Associate's Degree and am currently working on my Bachelor's Degree while raising my children and working. I will eventually work full time for a local center against domestic violence and hopefully, help other women reach their goals. I never thought that possible before, but now I dare to dream. **And dreams CAN COME TRUE!**

Several years ago there was another case in a small Tennessee town that did not end well. The father killed the mother and daughter and also shot the son. I fight for that family, whose voices have been silenced forever:

This is dedicated to Frieda and Rachel Elliot:

For the Silent Victims
For the victims lost forever
At the hands of one they'd feared
For the nights spent silently shaking
For the millions of fought-back tears
For the masks we're forced to wear
For the lies we have to tell
For the walks we take on eggshells
For the life we spend in Hell
For the women in the doorway
When at last the help does come
While the monster hides behind her
Out of sight – with a gun
For the children unprotected
Crying silent in the night
As their daddy hurts their mommy
And they are too small to fight
For the women still in fear
Scared to stay and scared to leave
For the ones who never made it –
For their families left to grieve

For the days I've almost given up
And crumpled to the floor
For the hands that reached to pull me up
And help me to stand once more
©2007 A. Martin

I wish I knew then what I know now. There are signs to watch for in abusive men which are often "ignored". Visit **www.health-first. org** for information on knowing the signs of an abusive partner and you can seek assistance from National Domestic Violence Hotline at 1-800-799-7233 (**http://www.ndvh.org**)

Today I Know It's True

By Amy Swoop

Today, I am the wife of a loving, godly husband, the mother of three beautiful daughters, and I am stepping into ministry ... stepping into Gods divine purpose for my life. Today, I tell you that my life is good. Today, I tell you that though I don't know where God will take me next in this incredible journey called *life*, I have hope. Today, I have solace. Today, I have peace that passes all understanding ... because today, I know Him.

Though I know that in this life there are mountains and there are valleys ... highs and lows ... ups and downs ... and that I am not exonerated from them, I also know that whichever one I face today, I will not face alone ... because today He is with me. But my life was not always like this.

As I approach 40, I can tell you that my young adult life was far, far from where I am now. My life was entangled in sin—sin that ranged from drugs to drunkenness to promiscuity—a lifestyle that compared to and was typical of my peers at that time.

The Christian influences in my life were my grandparents and my dear friend, Ann. Ann and I became friends in 5th grade, and we are still friends today—almost 30 years later. Ann often invited me to attend church with her. Her parents, also godly influences in my life, purchased my first Bible as a high school graduation gift for me. I now know it was the best gift I will ever receive. It was in that Bible that I searched for answers on the darkest day that I would ever know.

My darkest day occurred on Easter Sunday when I was 24 years old. My husband and I had only been married a year and were still living a party lifestyle. We did attend church, but only out of obligation to my mother-in-law. You see, I was living in two worlds: "playing church" but with no relationship with God whatsoever. I didn't know God. I didn't even know I needed God. I was in control ... or so I thought.

In high school, I had met Andy, who had become a dear friend. Andy was exuberant, full of life, funny, and a stylish guy. He was the brother I'd never had. We had connected the first time we met, and our friendship had grown and blossomed. We worked together; we played together. He was my husband's best man in our wedding.

Before my husband and I married, Andy and I had gone everywhere together; we were inseparable, but the relationship was totally platonic. You see; I do believe he was my brother. "My older brother," he would gladly and proudly proclaim.

On that particular Easter Sunday, Andy was to meet up with us after we had dinner with our families. As usual, we were late, so when Andy and our friend Lisa found that we were not at home, they decided to drive around and waste time until we arrived home. When we got home, we immediately received a phone call saying Andy and Lisa had been in a terrible car accident. We rushed to the scene where we found blazing lights and sirens, roads blocked, and lawns secured to form a landing pad on which the LifeGuard 10 could land.

Police told me we could go no further; we were not permitted near the accident. For years after that, I deeply regretted not busting through security to get to Andy one last time. Later we were told that his last words were concerning Lisa; asking if she was okay. Rescuers had placed Lisa in the ambulance and taken her to the hospital where she would receive numerous stitches in her head and arm.

My husband and I drove an hour to the hospital—a drive that I did not remember taking. In my mind, I knew it was bad, but I never could have imagined how bad. Never imagined how horrific it would be to see Andy hooked up to Life support. Andy suffered major head trauma, numerous broken bones, and a crushed pelvis—broken and battered beyond belief.

For three days I was in a prayer vigil. I camped at the hospital, refusing to leave and praying to a God that I had not known ... praying for someone—anyone—to save Andy.

Surgeons drilled a hole in Andy's skull to alleviate pressure on the brain through swelling—swelling that would finally cause his death. Three days after the accident his parents had no choice but to remove Andy from the machines that were technically keeping him breathing. As his brain function was diminishing, I asked to see him once more. I didn't know this would be my last visit with him. I went in and I told him to fight. "Fight Andy ... with all you've got ... fight," I said. I sat with him for awhile holding his hand, and when I got up to leave, he squeezed it. It was at that moment that I knew he heard me. In that moment, I thought Andy was telling me not to go, but now, I know he was telling me goodbye. Andy's parents wrestled with and finally agreed to organ donation and then two days later we buried him.

That was the darkest period that I had ever known. Young people aren't supposed to die. We still had a lot of living left to do. Andy was supposed to be here to know my children and be their "uncle." We were supposed to grow old together and tell our kids about the good times we'd shared. It wasn't supposed to be that way. *Why? Why?* I wondered.

When life resumed after the funeral, I became depressed. Not only was my best friend gone, but my husband's friend was gone, too. My husband could not fill that void for me, and I was so broken, I could not console him. We fought a lot, and all I wanted to do was sleep.

I went through the motions of life, but did not live. I dreamed vivid dreams of Andy—dreams of him, happy and alive, wearing his infamous rugby shirt and smiling. I was disappointed when I awoke and became angry—angry that I had been interrupted and awakened to the miserable reality of life. My dreams were happier than my reality. The dreams were so real and alive, just as I ached and yearned for Andy to be.

I recall on more than one occasion racing—physically running—to the mailbox as fast as I could, thinking that there would be a letter there from Andy ... thinking that somehow he really was not gone ... that his death was part of some cruel hoax. I was in such denial, and at times, I could barely function.

I remember looking for my Bible and asking, "Why?" I searched and searched. It was then that I found the scripture that says, "it rains on the just and the unjust."*What*"? I thought. *That's the answer—that there really is no answer? I thought all the answers were supposed to be here ... here in this BIBLE. Why would people lie to me?*

In the midst of all the torment and anguish, I composed three lines that are still with me today. The three lines said:

> *Save me from drowning in this sea of pain,*
> *Beacon to me your light of hope,*
> *That I may safely drift ashore.*

Those three little lines changed my life. I desperately wanted and needed relief. Help could not come soon enough. Those three lines were my cry for help to my Heavenly Father ... for I had nowhere else to turn. The pain was consuming me, just like the water consumes someone without a life preserver in a sea of rough waves. It was engulfing me and strangling me without giving me a moment of relief in which to catch my breath.

I continued to go to church and cried through every service every Sunday. After six months of grieving, I was so, so tired. Tired and sick; sick and tired. So one day, I decided to go to the doctor. I was in total shock when the doctors told us that I was expecting. *What? How?* We wandered through the ups and downs of nine months of pregnancy still in total astonishment. We later found out that my birth control pills had been recalled because they were defective. To this day, I still find that funny. They were recalled? "No, they were "God called." It was no mistake. God had orchestrated my pregnancy because He knew what our marriage needed for restoration ... for healing.

Andy's mom honored us with a baby shower, and our bond grew closer than ever. When we found out we were having a girl, we decided to call her Chloe, "our angel baby." In that birthing room, after her entrance in this world, I looked upon her face, and at that very moment I KNEW THERE WAS A GOD, AND HE WAS REAL. At that moment, hope was restored to our family. It was then that I BELIEVED; then that I knew I needed Him to be a part of my life. In later years, I accepted salvation, and I was baptized at 26. Our family continued to grow with the birth of two more wonderful daughters.

My husband and I became organ donors after we understood its importance and realized how many lives had been saved by Andy's physical body. And I cannot begin to tell you the scores of people that, as a result of Andy's death, were spiritually saved. I can account for four. In addition, my husband also rededicated his life to living for Christ. There is great, immeasurable comfort in knowing that my children will one day get to meet their "Uncle Andy" in heaven, for they have heard so many wonderful stories about him.

Today, I know that God knows me, my life, past, present and future. He knows where I am going and where I have been. He knows, He cares and He is with me.

"For I know the plans I have for you," declares the LORD, "plans to prosper you and not to harm you, plans to give you hope and a future." Jeremiah 29:11 (NIV)

Today I know that all things work for good for those who love the Lord, whether I understand it or like it.

"And we know that in all things God works for the good of those who love him, who have been called according to his purpose." Romans 8:28 (NIV)

Today, I know that what Satan intends for evil, God will use for good. Today, I pray daily to be the godly mother, wife, and woman that He wants me to be. I desire to know Him, follow Him, praise Him and most of all thank Him for allowing His Son, Jesus, to die on the cross, so that I may live; eternally.

Today though I may cry because I miss my dear friend, Andy. I rejoice that I will one day see him again. Today, I share my story to give you hope. Today, I want you to know that He is in control.

God does have a plan and purpose for my life and yours. There is hope beyond the pain, and though I have not always felt that way, today, I know it is true.

Love Doesn't Cost a Thing

By Robin Thomas

I am a 41-year-old single mother of three and although I still struggle, I am not the same person I was five years ago. I have been forever changed—changed not by myself, but by the power of God.

I was born into a dysfunctional family of alcoholics and grew up on a farm with my mother, stepfather, brothers, and step-siblings. My step-father was the only dad I ever knew, and he began to sexually abuse me when I was five. For many years, I believed it was normal. I thought all daddies did that.

We started going to church when I was eleven. When my Mom and Brother decided they were going to accept Jesus, I didn't want to be left behind so I decided to go along without knowing what it meant to have Jesus in my heart. I just went so I would not be left out. I had the head knowledge, but there was no heart knowledge.

Later in life, I accepted Christ as my personal Savior and began to study God's Word. I struggled for many years with the hidden sin that was happening in my home while my mother was working nights as a nurse who struggled with depression. I became scared when I saw her standing in the kitchen with a knife held to her stomach and wanting to die. I had no idea at that time that she had been raped on a date when she was sixteen.

When I was thirteen, my mother and step-father got a divorce, but I was still allowed to go over with my little brother to see him. The abuse continued, and when I was seventeen, I had my stepfather's baby. Yes, I did have the opportunity to get out of the abuse, but it was familiar, and I didn't know any different.

I was also abused by my step-father's uncle and a cousin. I remember thinking, *why am I here, and why is this happening?* But I never told anyone of the abuse until after I had my son.

Finally, I went to the Pastor of my church and told him what was happening. He said "I was afraid that was happening". He and his wife showed me unconditional love through this confession that I had been hiding for years but I still ran. I ran from God. I knew God had a purpose for my life, but it was easier for me to begin blaming the people in my life for all the things that were happening instead of reaching for God.

I married a man who was verbally abusive to me and conceived two children by him. We spent more time apart than together. He cheated on me while we were married and I believed that I was not worthy of having a good man in my life.

I finally got tired of not knowing if my husband would come home or not or who he had been with, so we divorced.

Through those years, I was miserable and spent my time in and out of counseling sessions, not having any idea on how to seek God for healing. I began to drink and take drugs allowing myself to be used by having sex with different men.

I also suffered with a food problem because when I was young my step-father had sent us to bed without dinner. This happened frequently and my mother would sneak food to us when she could.

In 1998, I met Dan—a man that was different than all the others. I moved 800 miles to be with him. Although I didn't know it, there was a purpose in it. Dan wasn't there to use me or abuse me. He helped me deal with many of my fears and hurdles. I had always thought that having sex with someone meant they loved me. Dan changed that wrong thinking. Although I was still running from God, God knew exactly where He was taking me.

In 2002, we moved to Tennessee because of Dan's job. In 2004, my children began going to a small Baptist church. They asked me to come and I went.

In 2005, I accepted Jesus into my heart and began a real relationship with Him. Life began to change for us as I began to give up bad habits and slowly let God have those parts of me that I felt were so bad. I also began to forgive all the people who had hurt me. I realized also that I needed to receive God's forgiveness for myself—which was very hard. Receiving God's forgiveness for my past mistakes has been the hardest thing for me to do. It is a conscious effort every day to hold my head up high and know that Jesus' blood has made me worthy. I am so thankful that my head knowledge has become my heart knowledge.

In April of 2007, we received news that my husband, Dan, had pancreatic cancer. That was another blow that I did not expect or know how I was going to make it through. But this time, I had a church family who loved on me and prayed for us. Dan had never accepted Jesus Christ as his Savior, so our Pastor came out many times to talk to him. I was concerned about what he believed and where his soul would end up. Dan accepted Jesus as his Savior one night while my church family was at our house. Thank You, Jesus!

I saw my husband go from being a very healthy man to just skin and bones. I was still thankful that I was there with him and we had Jesus in our lives. He died at 1:10 a.m. on Thursday, February 7, 2008. I was devastated.

Then Satan began speaking those lies: *"See, they leave you one way or another."* But even though I struggled, God was still holding me through that difficult time when I had lost my best friend and companion. God put another person in my life that had just lost his wife, and we leaned on each other.

Over time I realized that deep down I was angry that I was alone at 40 and began making poor choices that lead me into sin.

One night, a gentleman got up at our church and shared how he had been so angry with God for taking his son. I felt a wave of anger build up within me, and I thought, *"why God why"*? Then the verse from Jeremiah 29:11 came to my mind which says *"For I know the plans I have for you,"* declares the LORD, *"plans to prosper you and not to harm you, plans to give you hope and a future."* (NIV). God instantly gave me peace, and I asked for forgiveness for being angry and bitter.

I am so glad that God has brought me to where I am today. *"You have turned my mourning into joyful dancing. You have taken away my clothes of mourning and clothed me with joy,"* (Psalm 30:11 NLT)

I know that God has brought me through all of this to use me for His purpose. God comforts us in all our troubles so that we can comfort others. When they are troubled, we will be able to give them the same comfort God has given us. (II Corinthians 1:4)

I still hear that voice saying, *"You're not worthy; you will never be anything; you can't be used by God,"* but I speak to that voice "YOU ARE A LIAR!"

Jesus has made me worthy. I am His chosen daughter, and He is using me today. My plea to Him is, *"Create in me a pure heart, O God, and renew a steadfast spirit within me."* (Psalm 51:10 NIV). It is a daily renewing of my mind and heart.

I don't look back at what I have lost, but at what I have gained *"For I can do everything through Christ, who gives me strength."* (Philippians 4:13 NLT).

It is so important to read and study God's word. Our spiritual weapon to combat the lies of the enemy is with His Word. It is in those moments when you cry out to Him and He tells you that He was always there, even in all that ugliness and sin, that you receive freedom and peace. I am so thankful today for the freedom He has given me to walk in His love and mercy.

God Gives the Greatest Smile of All

By Janie Burkett

My name is Janie, and I could be your best friend, your neighbor, your sister. My story is about abuse, and it happens every 15 seconds in the United States. My story is about how my Savior saved me and gave me a voice to help others. He even had butterflies fly around me one time to show me I can fly and smile from the inside out.

As I sat and thought about my past, these words came to me: "You gave me 10,000 candles, and I gave you 10,000 smiles. I believe God spoke to me because I had candles lit all the time for comfort.

I was raised with parents who went to church whenever the doors were open. My mom was a Girls in Action (GA) leader and helped involve girls in the mission of God. She was into everything the church had to offer. My Dad was a Sunday and Wednesday father and enjoyed church as much as Mom.

My grandparents on both sides built a church in our home town and actively participated in most activities that took place there. They and my parents were all buried in the church cemetery. Needless to say, I grew up on the inside of that church, which is still going strong today. I accepted Jesus as a small child and immediately became committed to many church activities. I also loved showing my faith at school by carrying my Bible with me. These years of my life hold warm memories.

Growing up, I always dreamed of having a knight in shining armor, a white picket fence, and loads of children. I wanted a football team ... thank goodness God had other ideas!

I was married the first time for 11 years and gave birth to 2 wonderful boys. We moved around a lot and I fell short of the glory of God because I joined my husband in drinking to enhance our relationship. What a stupid mistake!

My mom and uncle finally talked me into leaving my husband after he turned to drugs and alcohol often leaving me and my 2 sons with no money for food or diapers. After I left him, I lived with my mom until I found a job and we divorced. Thankfully, my ex-husband and I have become friends with a working relationship. God is good!

I seem to have always had a problem with picking guys with bad tempers who drank and did drugs. I met my second husband on the street where I lived. He was a football player from my grade school class. Initially, he was great to my sons and wonderful to me, so I thought things would be good at last. Well, it wasn't. That marriage only lasted 6 months. I walked out when he came home drunk one night and attacked me and began to tear my clothes off in front of my sons. My sons tried to fight him off, but he sent them flying by hitting them. I walked out because he hit my sons, not because of what he did to me. Now I was twice divorced and still looking for that wonderful life.

As I worked and raised my sons and tried to get in the right steps again, I met a guy who was as cute as peanut butter and jelly. He was sweet, kind and his eyes just made me go right to him. We had our first date and that relationship lasted for 16 years. I never married him, because I figured I didn't do well at marriage. I thought marital failure was my fault. I thought if I just lived with him things would be okay. Sure they would.

My record of finding the right guy really was not good. I had high hopes, but I didn't have God. After my partner gave me the first slap, I tried to figure out what I did to make him so mad. As always, I thought it was my fault.

We got along good and we drank with the best of them. So what happened? I learned that no matter what you did with him or to him, his other face would come out. He had two faces: the good, mild, sweet one and the mean mean mean one.

I learned to drink to hide the pain. I never took drugs, but I would drink myself to a stupor until I passed out.

One night I was sleeping when he came home. I got up to see what he was saying, and I went to the bathroom. He followed me and told me to never walk away from him when he was talking. I felt his hand on my head as he pushed my head into our bathroom sink. I heard bones in my face and nose break. I looked up and saw my nose was split in half, so I got a band aid and put it across my nose to pull the skin together. I never went to the hospital because I never wanted anyone to know he was that mean. I wore sunglasses and long sleeves all the time to hide the bruises he gave me just about every day.

One time I was sitting in the living room watching TV and he and the boys were playing cards. He was in the den and pulled out a shot gun and fired it, just missing me in my chair. He said I was to get up and let him sit down, so I got up and went to bed.

I was planning to leave him while trying to sort out how to do it. I was afraid because he had told me if I ever left he would find me and kill me, my mom and my kids. We purposely moved to another state because he said I was too close to my family and needed to be away from them. Due to the violence I suffered, I believed he would really kill my family.

I had always told my mom and sister that things were great and we had no problems. I was a good liar because they believed me.

After an incident, I went to the hospital and the x-rays showed that every rib in my body had been broken, bones in my face had been broken, and my collar bone had been broken. They said that every bone in my body has been broken at some time or another. At that time I never knew anything about domestic abuse; nobody ever told me about that, and I had never been around anybody else that has been abused or willing to share their story.

One day, while I was at a store, a lady who was a total stranger, told me, "Honey, you do not have to put up with that! And I would just told her that I fell.

One night I was having a bad night and decided to empty all the beer in the house and throw it out. I wanted to stop drinking, so out it all went. He got so mad; he beat me to where I passed out for a few minutes. When I woke up, a shotgun was at the back of my head. I closed my eyes and prayed, *"Father, Thy will be done. I am too tired; it is in Your hands."*

I heard the click of the gun and knew he had tried to shoot it; but it never went off. I heard another click and again it didn't go off. He turned around and threw the gun, and it went off in the wall. He went to bed as if something had come over him. I had been beaten so badly that I moved slowly. I was sore from head to toe. I left and went down the driveway, never to go back. I knew my God had put His finger in that gun so it wouldn't go off. He had saved me. What an awesome God we have.

I have been kicked, thrown out of a car going 70 miles hour, beaten to where I thought I was going to die, shot at, and raped. Every bone in my body has been broken, and I have been thrown in jail over a lie he made up to show me he could have me put me in jail and there was nothing I could do. But he underestimated my Father in heaven ... my God, my Savior.

I looked in a mirror and said, *"God come back into my heart; take the drink away from me, and please make me whole again."* Crying, sobbing, and on my knees, I prayed to be whole again. I never took another drink, and I never looked back ... only forward.

You know, God has a really great sense of humor because He made me whole and put a voice inside me that was screaming to get out...a voice that said, "No More Abuse ... to me or anyone! I definitely never thought of myself as a public speaker, but God opened the way for me to share my story of abuse with over 600 doctors.

Meanwhile, the remaining physical scars were an offense to my deliverance from abuse. I wanted Mr. X's hands off my face. I needed to see in the mirror a redeemed, healed woman looking back at me. God led me to a doctor in North Carolina who could address this dilemma. The scar removal *"Face To Face"* program was in its trial stage and participants were sought. My face had been so disfigured from the abuse that the surgeon got lots of experience — and I got a new face! My Father was the real healer but He used that wonderful doctor to remove my violent past from my face.

I was also blessed to be a source of help to other women. My personal resources were so very low, yet the provision was always there when a woman reached out for help. He loves to make us His vessels of blessing.

By the grace of God I was able to move forward with my life. He showed me that no matter what I go through He is there with me. There was another way in which I was not alone. Many, all around me needed to hear my story and feel my touch of compassion and understanding. I could easily relate to those searching for a way out of their counter-productive life, and my experience gave them direction.

I had given up on men and had totally raised my sons. From my perspective, the Lord was my husband and that would always satisfy me. I did not feel uncared for or lacking in any way. Then, at my son's suggestion, a new desire began to take shape inside of me. Knowing that there are kind, godly men out there, I felt these words coming out of me, "*God, I know one day you will send a good man to me. I don't care what he looks like ... as long as he will be good to me and my family.*"

Sometime later I became friends with a wonderful guy who was so fun to be with yet was never pushy about our relationship. As my family's life took dips and turns — good and bad — he was always there, offering wisdom, support and friendship. I soon recognized that this man's love was pure and sincere, not fake or conditional as I'd found in all other men in my past. After ten years of friendship we were married. Being all I ever dreamed of in a husband, he is one of God's best gifts to me. He still makes me laugh. So, you see, God has been with me all the time. I just had to wake up and open my heart again to Him.

My words to readers who are suffering abuse are these: What you do with your life is up to you. You need God in your life and He is there for you. He will show you the way if you will call out to Him.

No one should be hit, hurt, abused, or threatened. No one should live in fear. Do not believe the lie that you caused this to happen to you. It is not your fault: Not the hitting nor the threats and insults. It is not normal and it is wrong to let it continue. If you have children, please know they feel your pain in a very unhealthy way, and they also live in fear. No matter what the situation, abuse is abuse, and no one deserves it.

God is with you to guide you, so open your heart and let Him in. He will guide you out of abuse. He is with you through it all, waiting for you to say, "I need you now, Lord." Walk with Him hand in hand, and you will smile ... and oh, what a smile it will be ... a smile that is from the inside out ... the greatest of all smiles. Let God give you that smile. I'm so glad I did!

For more information on the physician who helped Janie, visit http://www.cynthiagreggmd.com

Simply Too Much Talking

By Cheryl

The first time I said, "I do" was with a handsome young boy during a pretend ceremony that took place on an elementary school playground during recess. All of our classmates were there to witness the grand event. My best friend walked me down the gravel path to where he stood, smiling at me just as innocently as I was smiling at him. Everything was perfect up to the point of our hearing, "You are now husband and wife." But neither the daring, young groom, nor I, the beautiful autumn bride, were prepared for the next set of words: "You may kiss the bride." We giggled as we leaned towards one another, and I will never forget that half-a-millisecond when our lips were pressed together making our playground marriage official. Looking back, I realize that my grade school "wedding" became the formation of my dream of a perfect, happily-ever-after marriage.

My actual wedding day was anything but happy. The tears on my face, plus the emptiness I felt as my father escorted me down the aisle, reflected my gut feeling that this was no fairytale. A romantic interest in my groom had begun years before, but our romantic relationship was quite sporadic and shallow. After a very brief dating stretch he had convinced me of the benefits of living together. I knew this went completely against my upbringing, but I still agreed. The following two-year period presented some stormy times. Looking back I realize one big problem, although not apparent to me at the time: My groom did not believe in God or want any part of Him. For my part, I was keeping the God I loved as a child at a far distance. So without God present in our relationship, how do we correct our problems? Simple! Move onto the next logical step...Marriage!

We made a spontaneous decision to elope and had the entire wedding planned in six quick days. On the eve of our wedding night I was wishfully longing for a romantic gesture before we said good night, but I could not help but sense from him a complete emotional "shutdown." Why now? No, not on the night before the most important day of our lives! Not one longing look into each other's eyes, not one single discussion about our goals and dreams for the future, and most definitely not one single expression of affection. My fantasy of having romantic fairytale love story was quickly becoming my worst nightmare. With my pillow quietly absorbing each tear I began to realize that this marriage union was going to be business as usual...nothing romantically magical. With each round of tears came a plea from deep within asking if this is really how people live happily ever after.

The next day I was able to mask my tears of sadness as tears of joy and happiness. It all went down quickly and predictably. What should have been the happiest day of my life was simply turning into my cold reality of sadness. We immediately returned to our apartment. I continued teaching while my groom lost and found jobs. The honeymoon was already over; rather, it never really ever began.

Several months went by and then, unexpectedly, hope was restored. A bright pink plus sign for "positive" meant a chance for my husband's heart to melt at the sight of his very own child. As I joyfully shared the wonderful news, I waited patiently to see a smile of excitement! But, once again, I felt nothing more than an emotional "shut down" as he bluntly told me he didn't want a baby. His words ripped me to shreds, yet simultaneously a resolution jelled within: This was a gift of life from God growing inside me. Regardless of my husband's opinions I was completely thrilled! My new purpose in life was to love, provide, and protect my baby.

Nine months later our baby girl was born! While he was happier than expected, his attitude towards our marriage and family did not change.

So where does a young, heartbroken new mother go for sympathy? Simple! To her Daddy, of course! So I called my Dad! Did he offer me any sympathy? Not really. But he did listen intently through my tears about the anger and the confusion. Then suddenly, between sobs, he suggests that something might be missing in my life. He then asked me a series of questions that I felt were a bit off topic.

"Do you believe in God?" "Do you ever find a quiet place to talk to God?" "When you talk to God, do you ever stop to listen?"

Yes...Sometimes...and Listen? Now that's a new idea! Daddy's instructions were to talk to God, and then to simply listen to what He might want to say to me. Daddy explained that answers could sometimes be quite direct, could come through others, or even be shown in God's own unique and unhurried way.

I began talking to God, an exercise I had ignored for such a long time. I tried my best to listen, but my marriage was not improving. In fact, it became increasingly worse. The more I cried, the more I called my dad, and the more he steered me back to God.

With my new prayer habits in place, I could clearly see the distinction between my trust in God and my husband's disinterest in anything spiritual. We married for the wrong reasons, and God was never allowed a place in our union. I must admit that I was tempted to call for a divorce, but I was pretty sure that God would not approve. The last thing I needed was Him mad at me! I simply let God know why I was hesitant to ask for a divorce. I knew it was wrong, but I decided to stick it out. I told God I would do whatever He wanted me to do — then, as instructed, I stopped talking and simply listened. Not a single answer was heard. Not a single heavenly hint.

Before our third wedding anniversary, my husband announced that it would be best if we began divorce proceedings. He could not rationalize us continuing in a marriage that was filled with this much unhappiness. To him, it was simple...I wasn't what he wanted in a wife. For the sake of the child, he felt that the sooner we terminated this relationship the better so I could have a chance of finding true peace and happiness.

Was fear running through my veins at the realization that I would now be a single working mother of an eight month old baby? Absolutely! But, oddly, the fear was quickly replaced with the most calming peace felt deep within—a sensation that I had not experienced until that moment. The pain, the anger, the resentment... simply vanished.

After we settled into our new routine, I began to dream again about how wonderful it would be to find the kind of husband that God would want me to have. After asking God for his guidance to lead me to the right man...I listened. I then wrote a "Needs and Wants" list of the characteristics I desired in a husband. I wrote out a list with a dash of faith. I began to believe again that God had an amazing plan for me. I continued moving closer to my Lord by talking to Him often — and by faithfully listening. After I wrote the list I tossed up the idea of "finding" a husband up to God. I remember asking Him to send the right man my way when He was ready. Until then, I would begin dating without the intent of hunting down a husband.

An amazing fairytale story unfolds at this point. I met a wonderful gentleman and began dating. During our courtship, I was constantly in awe of how connected we were on so many different levels. One day I stumbled upon my original *"Needs and Wants"* list. The more I read the list...the more the hairs on my arm would rise! What made us both realize that God had been talking to us throughout this journey is that my friend had often prayed for Him to bring him the right girl in His own time. We both believed that we were recipients of a precious gift. Just as Daddy had said, *"sometimes answers come in God's own unique and unhurried ways."*

God answered our prayers for His blessing. We became engaged and had a beautiful church wedding among family and friends. Holding my Daddy's hand as we prepared to walk down the aisle he whispered, "I believe you found the right one this time." Reaching the altar, Dad said a quiet prayer, asking God to bless our marriage.

My husband and I are now seven years into our marriage. We face everyday challenges just like everyone else. I have no regrets of the past...simply more time to talk to God as we move forward in our journey together.

Listening to God is not always an easy thing to do. I'm still learning to listen to God. I admit...sometimes I talk too much and forget to listen. That's a huge mistake! It's like asking Jesus for directions, then driving off without waiting for His answer. When this happens, I usually find myself lost all over again.

Are you looking for help? Have you tried asking Him? You can ask Him about anything! Once you've said all you wish to ask or tell Him, simply stop talking and listen! As you learn to listen and look for His direction you will be amazed that He will always provide the answers you need.

Beauty for Ashes

By Anna Moultrie

I was a battered woman for twenty-one years. I married my first husband at the age of fifteen, but my marriage ended in 1988 when my husband, who was a violent alcoholic, was murdered. My life up to that time was characterized by constant fear. I felt like I was walking on eggshells because I lived with verbal, physical, mental, and sexual abuse. I was not allowed to have friends and had very little contact with my family. My life was controlled and manipulated, and I was made to think that I was totally worthless and a pathetic excuse for a woman.

In our seventeenth year of marriage, my husband's best friend married a woman who was also very controlling and manipulative. She allowed her husband little time for friendship with my husband, and my husband was not willing to have it that way. With much interference, my husband destroyed their union in little over a year. During that year, I gave birth to our first child.

During their marriage, my husband and I experienced several violent situations with this couple. The wife, who had taken a close interest in my baby girl, saw how tolerant and forgiving I'd become to my lifestyle. For some reason, my husband trusted her with our daughter, so she was able to stay somewhat close in our lives. Oddly, she always came around at my lowest times.

One day, after a really bad night with my husband, I called and asked her if she could come help me with my daughter. When she saw my condition, she became angry and shared her hatred towards my husband and her fear for my safety and my daughter's safety.

A couple years passed, and in 1988, I became pregnant with my second daughter. In the eighth month of my pregnancy, my husband left, never to return. A week after he left, his body was found, and I became the number one suspect in his murder. That was the beginning of my nightmare!

Four weeks later, I scheduled the delivery of my second baby daughter. My friend had been hanging around pretty much all the time.

The police questioned me a lot about my husband's death. Then they asked me to take a polygraph test. To their surprise, I passed. By that time, my friend had started giving me Zanex™, which she said were muscle relaxers. She insisted that I needed the medication to help me get some rest from all the stress that I was under during the murder investigation and from raising two small children. At her insistence, I began taking the medication and became addicted.

I decided to visit my family for Christmas for the first time in many years, and my friend went along to help with the girls. After a couple of days at my folks, they realized I had a problem. They got me alone and told me that my friend would not allow them to have any contact with their grandchildren. They had also noticed that all I did was sleep. I immediately stopped taking the pills. I confronted my friend, and she became enraged because I took my family's side over hers.

I flew her back to Georgia the next morning, and I stayed to visit my family for a couple more weeks. I then began to see for myself how much control I had let that woman have over my life and how out of control she was.

I moved back to Texas near my parents, and for a year, all was great. When my youngest daughter was six months old, God sent me a wonderful, strong, gentle, loving man—the man He knew I was going to need. We fell in love and were married.

Soon after my marriage, I got a surprise visit from my old friend. She told me I owed her for doing me a favor. I called my husband immediately, and we agreed that the problem was not going to go away. She contacted the FBI. After three weeks of taped conversations, she came out and said she wanted a sum of money. A meeting was arranged at the San Antonio airport, where she was apprehended for extortion.

Six months later, I was arrested for the murder of my first husband and extradited back to Georgia. A month later, I was released on bond, and for the following three years I lived a normal life. My friend confessed to the murder of my late husband, and my attorney arranged a meeting with her and my late husband's family attorney. At that meeting she asked to speak with me in private. She wanted me to financially support her while she served a life sentence. In return, she would tell everyone the truth that I had not had any knowledge of what she had done. When I refused, she told me to take a good look around because I would be sharing prison time with her. I sat in front of her, listening and watching, as she, with a straight-face, convincingly said that I had paid her to kill my husband.

My mother died unexpectedly in June 1994, right before my court date, which was later that month. At that time, my baby sister was on her death bed with cancer. My life seemed to be falling apart right before my very eyes.

When my day in court finally arrived, it became obvious that my attorneys had never intended to have a court hearing. You see, it was a political year and in that very small town, the district attorney didn't want to lose a case. His career was on the line. I was railroaded into a plea and given a ten year sentence, of which I was to serve three. My attorneys had learned of my battered woman syndrome and knew my weakness when it came to my children. They used that to get me to cop a guilty plea. I was looking at a life sentence and the possibility of never being able to raise my daughters, and I was scared. My late husband's attorney offered me a plea of ten years, to serve one year of it, if I would give up my parental rights. My answer was, "NO!"

During those three years I had made a life in Georgia with my daughters and husband, God had given me a wonderful church family and many wonderful close friends. The morning I was to leave to start my incarceration, my sister and my best friend came to embrace and comfort my daughters. After we had all hysterically said our goodbyes, my precious husband—dying a thousand deaths and being ever so strong for the both of us—drove me quietly for three hours to the jail. Within a couple blocks of the jail, he pulled off the road, reached over, and embraced me tightly for a short while. He then put my face in his hands and looking through tears told me to be strong. He assured me of his dedication and committed love and also assured me that God would hold everything together.

My baby sister died soon after I was incarcerated and was not able to attend her funeral.

God, however, used prison to bring about my ultimate healing from all the hurts, the false accusations, misrepresentation from attorneys, and separation from my children, my husband, and my family. It was a time when I gained confidence and self-esteem. God used my prison sisters in obedience to His voice to speak to me about my deceased husband and to forgive him for all the years he had physically, emotionally, and sexually abused me. Even though we were in a very guarded area, God moved mightily in my heart and in every area of my life for my ultimate and complete restoration. I was able to forgive the woman who falsely accused me of conspiracy to commit murder and who caused my life to be turned totally upside down. She is currently serving a life sentence for the murder of my husband.

Even as Christians, we cannot control every situation or circumstance, but we can control how we react to those times. The light of Christ shining through us is what draws others to Christ. God opened my heart to be sensitive to the needs of others around me. He used me to counsel, to witness, and to encourage not only my fellow inmates, but also some of the security officers. I was given favor by God, and He kept me safe and helped me be respected by all. My time in prison was an example of how God took a very hardened and untrusting heart and remolded it so that I could become a loving, sensitive, humble woman, mother, and wife.

Because I had detached myself from my family and friends to adapt to my prison environment, my return home was a difficult adjustment period for me and my family ... but we made it through and now love each other more than anything in the world. God has restored everything back to me and has given me *"Beauty for Ashes."*

Prior to and during my three year ordeal, my church family, friends, and loved ones gave me strength by standing with me with their prayers and letters. They even assisted with the needs of my children and family. My daughter's school was also supportive and reached out to my daughters with counseling and protection from others. God was in everything!

I am now living a wonderful and peaceful life with the ones I love, and I am grateful to my Lord and Savior for never leaving or forsaking me! He truly is my source and my peace.

The Prodigal Princess

By Julie Peyton

When did it happen? When did I go from "a good Baptist girl" to sinner of all sinners? I use that harsh term because that is how I viewed myself at a certain period in my life. It's not that I didn't know better. The difference between right and wrong was clear in my head. It just didn't always agree with the desires of my will and heart. Like most children, the forbidden was irresistible. It was worth checking out even if the result was terrible condemnation.

One of the seeming traps along the way was my personal experience of my grandmother's death. This brought a fear of the unknown that led to nightmares and distressful thoughts about loss. Eternity loomed out ahead like an enormous black sea that could swallow one up at any moment. Suddenly, Sunday School Bible stories were not sufficient to answer the mysterious queries of my terrified, ten-year-old heart. Real life was something different than what was presented to me as "answers."

Determined to equip me with a proper foundation, my mother ushered me down to the front of our church one Sunday for me to publicly accept Him as my Savior. Her precious heart was full of good intentions. *My* heart, on the other hand, lacked a sense of need for this salvation being offered me, and I was not at all prepared for the demands required to follow Jesus. The promise was eternal life — but I could not understand what that meant for me. I was pronounced "saved" without much understanding of how that might impact my life. I kind of stuck it in my back pocket and went on with life.

Life floated by, and I spent most of it on a bicycle, on the basketball court, playing Atari with my siblings, or giggling over first crushes with my best girlfriends. Age 10 evolved into 15, and somewhere in between I entered the age of reason. You know the age—where you say to your mom, "Give me one good reason why I cannot go?" and she says, "Because I said so."

In my great wisdom, "because I said so" was not good enough, so I thought I had no other choice but to find a way to do what I wanted to do, regardless. And so, began my downward spiral—a spiral that seemed to be set in slow motion. I was no longer the innocent little Baptist girl, and to be honest, I didn't really want to be. Was I ashamed? Yes, but at that point I felt like there was no other way to live.

At age sixteen I discovered I was pregnant. My life's dream was to be a wife and mother, which lent some comfort to my situation. The terror came with the thought of telling my parents, and what their reaction might be. At four months I could no longer conceal my secret. After initial shock and heartbreaking anger they moved on to love and concern. Though I could not recognize this as God's gift to me then, I was so very grateful for my parents' presence in my life at that time.

The baby's father was the love of my life. We were crazy about each other. By our fourth date we were talking marriage, even though high school graduation was still years away. Thus, it made sense to us to get married and legitimize this child. Three months later our son was born. It was "love at first sight" for both of us. I did hear the whisper of God as I stared at my new-born child, but I didn't know what to do with this strange, new sensation. Only later, in hindsight, did I recognize the Father's slow, deliberate process of transformation in my heart. Meanwhile, life was good. In fact, those first years of family life were truly among the happiest of my life.

But a honeymoon doesn't last forever, and soon the realities of life were pressing in upon us. The need to get caught up materially and to chase after career dreams pushed us to that fast-paced, high tension environment that was barely manageable. Then I got pregnant again, requiring me to cut back on various pursuits. Although our parenting skills were strong, our money management proficiency was horrible. Between that and a complicated birth of our second child, we soon began to feel the results of irresponsible spending.

Declaring bankruptcy became our only option, accompanied by huge doses of guilt and embarrassment. But God was so gracious to us. My learning curve vastly improved in tracking our spending and balancing the checking account. Then my husband landed a new job that almost doubled his wages. That was followed in time by the birth of our third child. The path of life was becoming smooth again. It was like we were given a second chance to get it right.

I was reminded of God's goodness during this time, and felt I owed it to Him to return to church or some form of organized religion. But it never worked out. I never could find the right spot for me. Besides, the God of my past held fear and uncertainty. So even though I turned away from Him once again, I know He never gave up on me. The vacuum that created in my heart set me up for the next big crisis.

A lie from the enemy was put to me through some friends with whom I associated. "Since you married young you have missed out on so much that life has to offer." Those initial tantalizing thoughts graduated to destructive desires to discover what I might have missed earlier in life. Suddenly this was my husband's fault. He stole my youth from me. Imagined deprivation soon moved to unabashed behavior, one bad decision followed by another. The fact that many of my peers were acting in the same way eased my guilt.

Our marriage was one huge train wreck. It was dead.

This was the bottom of the pit to which I had to sink before God could get my attention. There I was, battered and broken, with more regret, shame and fear than I could bear. I was literally sick of fighting my husband, fighting myself and fighting God. In total desperation I heard God calling me from beyond my darkness. And I called back, "God, please help me." The help I wanted was for my life to go back together like a repaired Humpty Dumpty. Meanwhile God had also been at work in my husband's heart, drawing him to Himself. The journey now seemed to turn back toward order and reconciliation.

Our marriage was being resurrected with new levels of love and appreciation between my husband and me. We both began to understand the character of God with new insight. God was on our side; He was interested in our well-being. This was God as I had never before understood Him — beyond any previous religious interpretation. He brought some of His special children into our life to "flesh out" the meaning of following Christ.

My husband's personal life began to change dramatically as he sought after God and actually *wanted* to go to church and serve Him. I began to see him shed old ways and habits, as if he were slipping out of a coat when he walked into a warm house. It was like he started becoming the person that deep down I always knew he was.

At first, I was a little jealous of his relationship with the Lord. I wanted what he had with God, but somehow, I did not think I was good enough. Who would want me?

God began revealing Himself to me more and more each day, and my focus began to shift from what was negative in my life to what was positive. I wanted to do what was right; I wanted to be good. But there was still one hang-up: I still carried the shame and guilt of my past life; the mistakes I had made and the sins I had committed. Finally, I was ready to be free from it once and for all. It was a desire to repent that God had placed in my heart. Almighty God broke my chains of captivity to sin and stopped my vicious cycle of always acting according to my feelings. My fears of death subsided in those moments when God answered my question, "Who would want me?" by whispering, "I do!"

I was totally undone. I found myself for three days in true, on-my-face weeping and brokenness before the Lord. God lifted my head and removed my blanket of guilt, and I was raised to walk in newness of life! Thank you Jesus! God rescued me, and I am sold out for the Lord! Out of reverence and love for what my God did for me—the wreckage He saved me from—I have set my heart to love and serve not only Him, but His people. Apparently that was His plan all along, because within two years of my total submission to God, I found myself becoming a Pastor's wife!

Through my service to the church alongside my husband the Lord began to reveal to me all the hurting and oppressed women who simply needed to realize they are privileged to the same kind of love and grace that I have received. In 2006, God birthed through me (with aid from some dear sisters of the faith) Fit for the King Ministries for Women. We proclaim freedom, favor, and forgiveness through a personal relationship with Jesus. This ministry has seen many hearts healed, many pasts forgiven, and many women learning to live in victory through the one and only Christ!

God has blessed us with 20 years of marriage, and our children are healthy and going strong! Of course, we have our fair share of struggles, and at times, heartache; but God is our strength and our portion … everything we need! Personally, I no longer see myself as the little Baptist girl, sinner, or even just a good little church girl. I was, am, and will now forever be a Daughter—*a Princess*—of the Most High and Revered King! My past serves only as a reminder and testimony of God's love, mercy, and grace for me! No, I am no longer a slave to my past … my Master is Jesus the Christ!

For more information on Julie and Fit For the King Ministries, visit www. fitforthekingministries.com

Does Anybody See Her?

By Shannan Duggin

When you think of the world in which we live in what comes to mind? Do you see the homeless person who is riding the city bus all day simply because it gives him a warm place to stay even if it is just for the day? Do you see the teenager walking down the side of road in the middle of day and wonder why they are not in school and if their parents know where he is? Do they even care? Do you notice your co-worker who just found out that her husband has been cheating on her and is now vomiting her lunch thinking if she were just a little skinnier he might love her and she would be enough for him? Do you see the father who leaves his two young children in the back of a car left running while he slips into the local gas station only to emerge with a case of beer under his arm while cussing to his wife on the other end of the phone? Or how about the girl on your daughters cheerleading squad who just found out that she is pregnant again and thinks that one more abortion really isn't a big deal. After all, the first two helped take care of a problem her boyfriend refused to deal with and it's not as bad as everyone says it is.

We don't have to look too far to see that pain and suffering is all around us. The ways in which many people seek to escape the pain often leave them feeling exhausted, empty and hopeless. From television, to food addictions, the internet, to "happy hour" at the corner bar, people are constantly looking for ways to quench a thirst that can truly only be met by one person. That one person is Jesus Christ.

Why then do we seek answers in everything else but Him? Often times it comes from the way we were raised or experiences we had growing up with or without the church. I was raised in church and as a little girl I went to church religiously. I can honestly say that I missed only two days of church in 18 years.

As I got older I began to dread going to church because I viewed it as more of an obligation, rather than an invitation to participate in something bigger than myself. It was more about religion than relationship, and by the time I left home for college I was bound and determined that I would spread my wings, assert my authority over myself and not go if I didn't feel like it. That also meant lying to my mom just to keep her off my case, but I knew that going through the motions was getting me nowhere, and that if God wanted to meet with me, He would let me know.

When I was 21years old I had decided that going to college 200 miles away from my parents really wasn't quite far enough and that 600 miles ought to do the trick. Coupled with naive dreams of making it big in the music industry along with an adventurous and free spirit, I ran a hundred miles an hour in the wrong direction!

Soon after arriving in Nashville, without knowing a soul, I quickly found myself attracted to the bright lights of the big city. Along the way I had made a few friends and after batting my eyes in several different directions was sure I had found Mr. Right. Despite the fact that I had convinced myself I would never meet the man I was going to marry in a bar, I threw caution to the wind and became heavily involved with a Disc Jockey who worked in, of all places, a bar.

Some of my new found friends were able to see, what unfortunately I could not, and gently tried to steer me towards a slightly less perilous lifestyle. However in my infinite wisdom I was certain that I had things under control. Never mind the fact that I was spending 5 nights a week in a bar, I was driving home drunk, or that I was engaging in unsafe sex with a man who struggled with commitment. What I didn't realize is that I was seeking to quench a "thirst" that only one person could fill.

I managed to find a church pew every now and then partly from guilt, but mostly because I knew my mom would ask if I went to church and I hated to keep lying to her. I even had a couple of friends invite me to try their church. However since it was an invitation to a different denomination from what I was raised in, I quickly poo pooed the experience. Raising hands and shouting Hallelujah was a bit much for me and besides I didn't need more rules and condemnation.

Once again I reasoned that if God wanted to speak to me He would let me know. And He did!

After two years and many tears later, it had become painfully obvious that I was right. I really wasn't going to find my future husband in a bar, and that included the Disc Jockey working in the bar. I had been living with him for a couple of months trying to get on my feet and it was during this time I had come to the stark realization that he was Mr. Wrong.

I found myself lying, stealing, and constantly enduring pressure from him to use drugs. I was certain he was cheating on me, yet it took the harsh words of a woman I was working with at the time before the light finally came on.

I'll never forget that day I was boo hooing about the predicament I had found myself in and was hoping she would offer me a pat on the back and a word of encouragement telling me everything was going to be okay. Instead she looked at me straight in the face and said "You realize that you're just prostituting yourself don't you? Can't you see he's using you?" It took the wind right out of me. I didn't want to believe her, but everything in my spirit knew she was right.

I immediately took steps to secure my own place and planned to cease all contact with him as soon as I moved out of our apartment. Unfortunately it was a little too late. The day I signed the lease on my apartment, I totaled my truck and a week later I found out I was pregnant!

If God was trying to get my attention...He had it now. I was ready to talk and I gave Him an ear full, *"God I'm sorry, please, please forgive me. Why would you let this happen to me, what did I do to deserve this? I suppose you're just punishing me and teaching me a lesson? God I promise I'll be good from now on. I'll do whatever you want. Please God just make this problem go away"!* But in His infinite wisdom, God answered with a big resounding NO!

I knew I could not tell my parents I was pregnant, they would either kill me or disown me. I knew telling my boyfriend wasn't an option, he'd just ask me to get an abortion. So there I was scared and alone. The only person I could think to turn to was a friend who had invited me to church.

She supported me and prayed for me, but more importantly she invited me into the body of Christ. Immediately I was surrounded by Godly women in a mom's group that never judged me, but extended to me the grace that was present in their own lives. It was through a friend who looked past the scarlet letter and a group of women that withheld lofty glances and judgment that ultimately opened up the door for me to receive God's grace.

Ten years later and I can see the Lords plans for me and they are full of hope. Jeremiah 29:11 (KJV) says *"For I know the thoughts that I think toward you, saith the LORD, thoughts of peace, and not of evil, to give you an expected end."*

I am grateful now that God didn't just "make my problem go away". It is because of my son that I met my husband and now also have a beautiful daughter. It is because of my son that I was able to discover a relationship with Christ beyond the confines of religion. And it is because of my son that I am believing the work of Jesus will be continued to reach his biological father.

The Bible tells us in James 1:22 (KJV): *"But be ye doers of the word, and not hearers only, deceiving your own selves".* If you are like me and have spent the majority of your life thinking that just showing up to church qualified you as having served God, then you are not alone. While just showing up to church qualified me for good attendance it made me "merely a hearer of the word" and not a doer. I was deceived to think otherwise.

1 Peter 4:9-10 (KJV) says: *"Use hospitality one to another without grudging. As every man hath received the gift, even so minister the same one to another, as good stewards of the manifold grace of God".* I realized that God has placed in each one of us a gift for the very purpose of

serving those around us and by acknowledging the gifts He has placed in us we are better prepared to be active doers of the word and to be an instrument of God's Grace. Never have I seen this demonstrated more clearly than in my own life.

When I look back on my life, I am able to see the hand of God at work. After all these years of misperception about church, I am finally able to understand that the church is not limited to the building, but goes much deeper, as the living, breathing body of Christ that can eternally affect the lives of those around us.

I want to encourage you through my personal story to begin to look at those around you in your everyday life. I challenge you to be ever mindful of the people God places in your path and to view each person as an opportunity to express the love of Christ in a tangible way. You never know you may be able to help that girl or woman running a hundred miles an hour in the wrong direction just like me!

Life Beyond Regret

By Jami Sims

Falling leaves and fall festivals are sure signs that autumn has arrived. Every year our church hosts a Fall Festival, and every year we anticipate this fun-filled event. This year, to our delight, we had a new attraction, the monstrous slide, brother to the famous moonwalk.

Children climbed furiously to reach the pinnacle so they could feel the wind in their hair and butterflies in their stomachs as they plummeted to the bottom. My four-year-old son, James, was no exception. He literally could not take his eyes off that slide.

"That one, I want to go on that one," he insisted. So he went. His older sister, Madelyn, carefully helped him up the swaying path to the top, but just as they reached the platform from which they would slide, James obviously looked down, realized how high off the ground he was, and quit moving forward. His little body began tugging against Madelyn's helping hands. I could see the agitation in her face and the fear in his, but there was no turning back. The only way down was to slide.

Oh, how I wanted to rescue my all-too-eager son, but I felt helpless. Gently but firmly, Madelyn grabbed him and they began the two-second free fall down the breath-taking slide and it was over almost before it began, but James was not happy!

The next morning as we discussed the previous night's events and attractions, James told me that the Fishing Booth was his favorite. Madelyn said she liked the slide. *"Did the slide scare you a little, James?"* I asked. *"No,"* he replied. I was surprised by his response, so I didn't say anything. A few moments later James announced, *"It didn't scare me a little bit; it scared me a lot!"*

I laughed to myself as I thought about the honesty in my son's reply. As I thought about his scary little experience, I was reminded of a time in my life when I felt trapped and scared—not just scared a little bit, but scared a lot!

Lured by the promise of love and acceptance, the "fall festival slide" in my life was pre-marital sex. I insisted on taking a chance and quickly found myself at the top of a very tall slide looking down—terrified of what I saw. I wasn't looking down at the ground; I was staring down at two blue lines. The pregnancy test was positive. Paralyzed by fear, I saw the harsh reality of pre-marital sex. The "slide" didn't seem so attractive and alluring now. I wasn't just scared; I was petrified!

Like many others who have walked in my shoes, I didn't welcome the idea of aborting my child. However, the idea of pregnancy scared me, and abortion presented itself as the only option. Panic superseded rationale. I remember making the call to the abortion clinic as if it were yesterday. With my stomach in knots, I scheduled the appointment. Then, I waited, and waited, and waited.

Those weeks were agonizing. I knew I was violating my own moral code, yet, the fear of exposure, the fear of someone finding out that I had gotten pregnant, drove me to abort. I was focused on my immediate needs and did not consider the future. Emotions of that sort are difficult to explain and even more difficult to feel.

My view of abortion had always been conservative—abortion is wrong; it is murder. All that changed, however, when I faced an unplanned and unwanted pregnancy all my own. Then, thoughts such as, *This will be an easy way out … a way to not have to deal with my problem … no one will ever know,* replaced my conservative view of abortion. It's scary how personal experience can either strengthen or weaken character, values, and morals! For me, it was obviously the latter. Everything I thought to be true about myself came crumbling down all around me.

I must have lived those weeks surrounding my crisis vicariously, because looking back I remember nothing of making a sound, informed decision. There was no information; no alternative. Yet, conversely there was no voice of objection—no voice crying out for the innocent life of my child, save the brave protestors at the clinic ... but by that time, it was too late.

Cowardly, I entered the front door of the abortion clinic to end the life of my child, and after the procedure was quickly ushered out the back door. I was sent on my way with no understanding of what had occurred to my body, heart, soul, and spirit during those brief moments I lay on the sterile table of an abortionist. I bought the propaganda—abortion is the easy way out—hook, line, and sinker.

I chose to cope by separating myself from my abortion and numbing myself to the world around me. But the easy way out wasn't so easy anymore. Guilt and shame engulfed me, and like an open sore, pain oozed from my soul. I longed for forgiveness and a chance to go back and undo what had been done. The old saying that two wrongs don't make a right is so, so true. How could I have been so foolish?

Fear over the emotions I was experiencing, or better yet, trying not to experience, led to further separation and denial. I struggled to carry on with life and leave the past in the past. A part of me stuffed the pain deep down inside. I don't think I consciously chose to forget it, but subconsciously I removed myself as an active player in the decision I had made to abort. I told myself that I didn't do it. I convinced myself that it had not been me who had entered that abortion clinic ... It couldn't have been me ... I would never have done something like that. My pursuit to avoid the truth at all costs devoured my conscience.

Life after my abortion didn't change much from the life I had lived prior, yet somehow, I had developed a dead feeling about my life. I was a white-washed tomb, a newly painted house whose structure was rotting away. From all outward appearances, I was okay; but on the inside, the truth was screaming to be told ... to be heard.

"Help me! My heart cried out. "Oh, please love me ... I know I'm not easy to love ... I don't deserve love ... but please, someone please help me." I needed to be forgiven. I needed my innocence restored. I needed to know Jesus. But instead of embracing Him, I permitted a roller coaster ride of emotions to lead me further and further away from

the One true source of love. Before long I was back at square one—pregnant again.

Could this be my second chance? Those were not the words that immediately entered my mind as the test revealed I was going to have a baby, but they were the thoughts of my heart as news of this pregnancy began to take root. This baby would be my redemption ... my atonement child.

Scared half to death, I shared the news with the baby's father, who had recently moved clear across the country to embark on a new life. He wasn't excited, but neither was he breathing down my throat to have an abortion. Relief! Although, he was not physically present with me, his calmness about our situation set me at ease.

"We'll get through this," was his answer. We talked of marriage. I begged him to marry me, and I think he really wanted to; but he was scared. He wanted to do what was right, but now he was the one on top of that *"slide"* looking down—terrified of what he was seeing.

Days turned into weeks and weeks turned into months. I only saw him two or three times during my pregnancy, but when the time came for the baby to be born, he returned. He was a proud papa the night our daughter, Madelyn, was born. Love beamed from his eyes as he looked down at the bundle of joy he was holding in his arms. God's gift of life was ours, and we were proud parents ... but shortly after her birth, he left.

My sheer delight over Madelyn's birth was overshadowed by brief moments of torment from my past. I could not escape my past. I could not escape the fact that I was alone. Everywhere I turned, no matter how far or how hard I ran, it was always there: abortion ... loneliness ... alcohol ... neglect. The vicious cycle was once again spinning.

During my pregnancy the God of my childhood had been calling to my heart, *"Come back to Me, Jami, I love you!"* Oh, how I wanted what God had for me; but I was scared! I knew I would have to give up everything to follow Him. My grip was tight, and I could not let go of the sin that held me prisoner.

How can God forgive me? I wondered. *How can I forgive myself? What in the world am I doing to this sweet and precious child of mine? Will my life ever be "normal?" Is this how I am going to live for the rest of my life? Oh, God forgive me!*

Several years of living it out at the bottom of the barrel was enough for me. I was tired of running, tired of hiding, tired of doing it my way. It was the darkest time of my life, and looking back, the only way I can explain how my life changed is G-R-A-C-E! God used an extraordinary set of circumstances to call me back to Himself.

In January of 1999, I gave my life over to the Lord. I climbed into my Savior's lap and braced myself for the free fall down the "slide." For indeed, those first few years felt much like a free fall. I had been married for all of two months to a man I barely knew (who was not a believer), and I was again pregnant and still very insecure because of my past. But isn't God good? He blessed my feeble offering. My faith was small (I'm sure it was smaller than a mustard seed), but my God was gracious. In the spring of that same year, my husband, Brad, received Jesus as his Savior and became the leader, protector, and provider of our little family.

Easy? Not a chance. I fought Brad's attempt to lead every step of the way. Although my heart had softened to Christ, it was still rock hard to those closest to me. Brad didn't know much about my past, and I wasn't offering up any details. Our relationship before marriage had not been characterized by purity, and he knew that I had not been innocent by any means. He just didn't know how guilty I was!

My walk with the Lord did not silence my past. It was still there haunting and taunting me. But God allowed people into my life who would help pull me from my self-protective shell. He put me on the path to freedom, although it seemed that for every one step forward, I took two steps backward. At times, I thought the pain of the past would ruin my marriage and leave me crippled for life, but God continued to whisper words of hope in my ear.

Finally, the time came for me to tell Brad the truth about my past. He needed to know, but I was so scared to tell him. I feared I would see his disgust as my secret was revealed; but as I told him, I only saw love. He didn't say much, and I knew he was hurt—hurt deeply ... but he still loved me. What a beautiful picture of the love of Christ?

Working through denial, anger, and bitterness, and then extending forgiveness to myself and accepting the choice I made to abort brought wholeness to my broken heart. Freedom didn't come over night, nor did it come easily, but if you ask me if it was worth it, I'll tell you, "Absolutely!"

God has radically changed my life, my heart, and my vision. I am no longer a tattered woman searching for love and trying to make up for the past. I am a much-loved daughter of the King … restored and redeemed. I am a virgin bride clothed in robes of righteousness.

What happened to change my vision? God opened my eyes to the sin in my heart. He sounded the call to repentance, and I humbly responded. God made me new. He redeemed and restored me. II Corinthians 5:17 (NIV) states, *"Therefore, if anyone is in Christ, he is a new creation; the old has gone, the new has come."* God gave me a new vision of who I am in Him.

I **recognized** what Christ had done for me. Jesus paid the price for my sin. Oh, what an amazing and marvelous thing! While I was still a sinner, Christ died for me. (Romans 5:8).

Isaiah 43:18-19 (NIV) declares, *"Forget the former things; do not dwell on the past. See, I am doing a new thing! Now it springs up; do you not perceive it? I am making a way in the desert and streams in the wasteland."* Without a doubt, God took the wastelands of my heart and made them into babbling brooks.

I **realized** who I was in Christ. I quit conforming to the world's view of who I was. Transformed by God's Word, I found renewal (Romans 12:2). God's perspective of who I was in Christ transcended my thoughts and feelings of who I was. I am a treasure in the Father's hand.

I **revere** who I am becoming in Christ. I am striving to live in purity before my Father. Ephesians 1:4 (NIV) says, *"For he (God) chose us in him (Jesus) before the creation of the world to be holy and blameless in his sight."* Confident of His work in my life, I press forward to attain the goal to win the prize for which God has called me. (Philippians 3:14) God is still hard at work in my life, and just as He promises in His Word, His work will be continuous until the return of Jesus. (Philippians 1:6)

The enemy wants me to run from my Redeemer, and for years, I did. The bonds of sin were thick around my soul. But Christ broke the bonds. He set this captive free!

Over the years, I have learned much … lived much … fallen much … failed much; but most importantly, over the years, I have been **loved** much. (Romans 8:38)

Today, as God has brought beauty from ashes in my life and Brad's, we are happily married (much like newly-weds) with seven beautiful children and one on the way. Madelyn, my first born, has an incredible relationship with her dad (whom our family prays for on a daily basis to come to the saving knowledge of Jesus Christ), and my oldest son, Micah, is in heaven, where I will one day hold him and tell him just how much I love him.

*Jami Sims is the founder of Abounding Grace Outreach Ministries. She is the wife of Brad and the mother of eight precious children. Jami's desire through the ministry of Abounding Grace is to encourage others to find healing and freedom in Christ. For further information about Abounding Grace Ministries, please visit Jami's web site, **www.abounding-grace.com.***

.

The Right Man

By Rose Embler

I know now that God has always loved me — but I have not always felt that way. There was a time in my life when I did not like God because when I needed Him to protect me, He didn't. In fact, I believed that He didn't even know I existed nor seemed to be on my side. Besides, what did I need with one more man in my life?

My parents were the best. They were wonderful shepherds in my life and had no idea what happened when the adults all decided to go out for the evening, leaving the oldest boy cousin to babysit the rest of us. For some reason he singled me out for "special attention," directing the others to go on to bed. Although we did not have sexual intercourse, he used me in crude ways to spend his sexual energy. I was nine years old and I didn't know how to rid myself of the guilt and shame with which I was left. I didn't tell my parents because he had convinced me they wouldn't believe me. I didn't realize then that in leaving them out of this horror, they lost their power to protect me.

This is the first time I ever remember praying to God. I didn't know much about Him because we were not the church-going family and I was hoping He could fill in where my parents left off.

Sometime later another boy cousin was at the house. We were remodeling our home and my parents ran to town for supplies. There was cousin, standing in my bedroom, remarking on my beautiful womanly shape. With my resistance in full gate, he was on top of me in seconds. After raping me I threatened to tell my mom. He countered that he would say I asked him for it. It was over about as quickly as it started — but I was never the same.

The issue of sharing my secrets with Mama haunted me. I really wanted to run to her for help, but what if she believed I had asked for that encounter? How would I convince her otherwise? I would never want her to think that of me and I would never want to hurt her. So I kept the secret to myself, even though there were other sexual events during the next few years. This, I discovered later, was a huge mistake.

Female problems cropped up in my early teen years, so Mama took me to the doctor. He asked if I was sexually active, and, with Mama by my side, I flatly denied it. After an examination he suggested to my mom that she get me on birth control. Mama's livid anger toward me hurt deeply, but I still couldn't bear the thought of telling her the truth. In my heart I was convinced my cousins were right; she wouldn't believe me. Suddenly I was on the wrong side of my parents. I could not really get my mind around it, but I had lost the trust of those who loved me most on earth. It was a huge loss and because of this, I gained enough spunk to stand up to my cousins, so they left me alone.

By my 14th year the shy family girl bloomed into a rebellious, wild filly. I also had "real" boyfriends. Somehow the roughest, rowdiest boys found me. I became very popular among that type for all the wrong reasons. If a guy wanted sex, why not? He would probably just take it anyway — and what purity did I have left to protect? One boy in particular seemed like my special guy and we managed a decent relationship for almost three years. When I discovered his unfaithfulness I experienced another level of male betrayal. As a senior in high school, a bunch of us decided on a *"creek party"* one night, very remote from town so that no one would discover us. Most of our parents had no clue of this, as we had told them other stories to account for the very late hours. An older guy became my date by popular consent of the group. The party ended when everyone left but my date and me. This wasn't the plan and I was uncomfortable alone with him, especially in his drunken condition. But there we were, at his pick-up truck on a very cold night. He wanted sex and the deal he struck was that I couldn't get inside the warm truck unless I agreed. What blackmail! Just like a guy to force his passion on me when my options were down. Submission to that deal hurt me all over, from the soul out. I began to despise men and started to believe I would never find *"the right man"* for my life.

Never completing my senior year, I got a job and moved out on my own. I wanted to be by myself — and I couldn't imagine what my parents thought of me by now. We didn't communicate much at all anymore. A co-worker at my job bragged to me about her boyfriend. Later she and her guy called asking to come over to my place — and could they bring a friend with them? Fine with me. Both the guys seemed flirty in a nice way, but there was something a little different about them. Soon they all confessed: These friends are not guys at all! I froze! I noticed that they didn't act boorish like most the guys I knew. They began coming over regularly and in time the "friend" and I became a couple.

We lived together in a same-sex relationship for five years. I chose to relocate, hoping my parents would not learn of this turn of events. I had already broken their hearts and it was beyond me to destroy them any further. Though deep inside I judged this relationship as wrong, it brought me to a place of safety: A mutually loving relationship with no man to mistreat me! However, once again my trust was betrayed when I discovered my girlfriend's infidelity. Now I was back where I started: Totally devoid of anyone who cared a whit about me and my past a shambles. With a same-sex relationship I had crossed an unthinkable line, hoping to finally experience my needs met. I have no desire for women; I just wanted to be loved with no strings attached. Boys began to hurt me at the age of nine and young men were not working out for me either. The enemy knew what was happening in my life and was always lying to me. He had me right where he wanted me. I was weak, scared, abused, lost, confused, and depressed. I didn't know where to turn or who to turn too. However, I did know that if I was in a relationship that I had to hide, then there was a reason that I should not be in it.

Only a few days later I met a man in a bar who seemed to be kind
and patient. For three months of dating I was able to postpone sex
with him. This was not about any personal values either. I simply
hated sex because it was always taken from me. In time I discov-
ered I was pregnant. When I told him the news he informed me that
he was married but separated. The baby news seemed to please him
because he shifted into celebration mode: making the rounds at bars,
begging me to join him. When I wouldn't be his "bar girl" anymore
the kindness left my kind man. In a drunken stupor he beat me up,
abandoning me from home and my personal effects. Though he later
came begging for pardon, by then I had faced the fact that he was just
another double-crossing man — in the game purely for his own pleas-
ures! I wished right then I could kill every man in sight.

Oh, the shortness of my memory! The store where I worked was
being rebuilt by a construction crew and in walked the best looking
man I ever laid eyes on. He winked at me and I melted. It was instant
appeal on my part and I created reasons to be near the workers as
often as possible. Every time he came in he would simply wink at me,
never saying a word. Finally he asked me to dinner with him. It was
a wonderful, safe occasion, but I knew, with a pregnancy in place, I
could not allow this relationship to foster. Rather than trust him with
the truth I concluded that we should not see each other again — and
we went our separate ways. If he was as wonderful as my spirit told
me he was, he would never accept my current "complications" and my
sordid history. I was *not* a nice girl and I'd rather this handsome man
never know how *not* nice I was!

But he was not a quitter. He called saying he was coming over.
Over my resistance, he came — and we talked. Every ugly detail came
out, including my pregnancy. He only reassured me that I was now
ready to genuinely fall in love and that he wanted to be the object of
that love. Wow! What kind of man is this? Can I trust him? And can
I be trusted to be a good wife to him?

At this point I was not a Christian. I didn't exactly hate God —
but I had no use for Him because life had taught me that I could not
trust Him. Mr. Handsome and I were married, yet my heart remained

empty and lonely. One day in the midst of an argument I threw something at him in anger. I was so full of rage and he left the house to put some distance between us. Alone in the house, the moment of truth burst upon me. It was time for God and me to do business. On my knees I began screaming at God, *"What is it? Why did you give me a good man and still I want to pinch his head off? Why do you hate me? Why were you never there for me? Why didn't you protect me?"* In total brokenness I clearly heard Him speaking back. *"You are expecting your husband to fill a void in you that only I can fill!"* That voice was so apparent I looked around to see who might be standing there. In silence I wondered, *"Is THAT what it is? Are YOU what's been missing all this time?"* He assured me that His protection was there all along: From diseases, unwanted pregnancies and addictions — and too many other evils to name here.

I realized that this encounter meant a visit to church. I went, and cried the entire time. *"Do you not know that the unrighteous and the wrongdoers will not inherit or have any share in the kingdom of God? Do not be deceived (misled): neither the impure and immoral, nor idolaters, nor adulterers, nor those who participate in homosexuality, nor cheats (swindlers and thieves), nor greedy graspers, nor drunkards, nor foulmouthed revilers and slanderers, nor extortioners and robbers will inherit or have any share in the kingdom of God".* 1 Corinthians 6:9 (AMP)

This scripture was an eye opener for me and how the relationships I was choosing were wrong and caused unnecessary destruction in my life. The people that I knew that were living this lifestyle would always try to convince me differently by twisting scripture to make that lifestyle seem acceptable in God's eyes. I knew in my spirit that something had to change and it had to change quickly.

The following Sunday I went back to church and cried through the whole service again. The Pastor, sensing my need, invited me to ask Jesus into my life. I said YES! I can't begin to relate the awesome process of restoration and renewal that begun in me that day. It's like I have my real life back, yet much, much more. I am so grateful that after I accepted Christ Jesus to be my Lord and Savior and repented for my past sins that I knew my life would be different. I was truly forgiven and all my sins have been washed clean. Yes, I have been washed clean as white as snow!

The good news is that my earthly father and I are on the best of terms, my husband adopted that little girl I was carrying and has been the best husband and father for eleven years. What's more, with my past gone, God has allowed my gifts to flourish in serving others and encouraging young people to walk closely with their Lord. I have even been privileged to go on a mission trip to another country, helping people understand how much Jesus loves them.

I want to tell the world about Him. He is real — and He is a life-changer. He is the Man of my dreams; the Man my hungry soul needed to finally come home. The psalmist wrote, *The LORD preserves the simple; I was brought low, and He helped me and saved me."* (Psalm 116:6 AMP) In a statement, that is my story.

"My Child, Get Up"

By Kelleen

At the birth of my first child almost 16 years ago, it was discovered that I have O- blood type. This type of blood can be given to anyone no matter what their blood type, and only 7% of all people have it. Needless to say, I was on the American Red Cross radar!

I began giving blood every three months or so soon after, and honestly believe that the techs would have come to my house to get me if that meant I would donate. Say O- and they salivate. Every time there was an opportunity, I was there and with anyone else I could convince to come with me. Naturally, several years ago when my church had a blood drive, I showed up. A few weeks after donating I received a letter in the mail. The letter said I had tested positive for HIV and to get my life in order, I only had a short time before I was going to die.

My first thought was disbelief. I had never used drugs or had a sexual life that put me at risk. As the words, "you are going to die" kept echoing around in my head I slowly slid to the floor and asked God, "is this how it is going to end after a lifetime of survival". Then, peace enclosed around me like my favorite, comfy blanket and I said, "Thank you, Lord, for what you have given me the past ten years". I was scared and angry later, but my first thought was "Thank you".

As I reflected on my life and those precious recent ten years, I could not help but be completely overwhelmed at the mercy of God and all the blessings He has poured on me. You see, I was not raised by Godly parents, and mine were not just ungodly, my family life was absolutely mixed up crazy. My parents' tumultuous relationship mimicked a rollercoaster. My mother, freshly graduated from high school, fell in love with a tall, dark, and handsome police officer. They were quickly married and quickly divorced. Then back in love again and remarried only to divorce a second time, all by my fourth birthday. I never saw him again.

As a child, my mother often told me I was "a handful", and I am sure she did not mean that to be a compliment. From about age two (so I am told), I would have temper tantrums and throw myself on the floor, kicking and screaming to get my own way. My poor mother would not know how to handle me, and knowing my mother's personality verses mine, I can honestly say, she never stood a chance against my strong will. Perhaps for "backup", but certainly not for love, she soon married a third time and moved my brother and me far away from city life in Illinois and every family member we knew, to rural Arkansas. And I do mean rural, "you might be a redneck if" territory. Population: less than 500.

This town had no traffic lights, no police officers, and only one grocery store/ gas station that still sold penny candy in barrels. We went to the post office to get our mail, given to us at painfully slow speed, with a smile and the latest gossip by an ancient postmistress. To ask, "Why", got you a whipping for being sassy. Abandoned cars and dreams decorated the yards; walls of fear fortified discouraged hearts. Into this environment we were transplanted. His kids, her kids and their kids, combined into a family of 7: 4 boys and 1 girl. Ours was a house, but was never a home, full of anger and completely void of God or love. Perhaps it was her lack of faith, loneliness after the move, or just her disposition, but by the time I was six, I had front row seats to my mother's first of many mental breakdowns.

I was allowed brief moments of sanity. Summers were spent in loving companionship of my grandfather and grandmother. They would arrive the last day of school and collect me, returning to Illinois until the day before school began again in September. Oh, how joyful and peaceful those times were, full of silliness, laughter, and new adventures, and how I cried when I had to return home. For several years I had them all to myself, and boy was I spoiled. I soaked in that love and saw what normal, good, God fearing people looked like. Then my grandparents moved within a two hour drive from us. Wonderful? No. Now whenever I got to see them, the train wreck that was my family came along, and my mother's mental and physical health devoured whatever time and energy my grandparents had. I cherished the visits, but there was an interruption in the connection.

I can appreciate a lot of things I learned as a result of my childhood. Before I was 10, I was driving the old GMC pickup truck with faded red paint down washboard gravel roads, fearlessly jumping terraces in the cow pasture on motorcycles too big for me to drive, learned to shoot on a 30.6 rifle, and I could fillet a catfish so thin what was left was transparent perfection. I knew just where to look on a hot summer day to find a fresh water spring where you could stop and get the sweetest, coldest drink of water, and how to trek through the woods, killing snakes along the way, always finding my way home. The only thing I could not seem to do was wear shoes. To this day, you will find me barefoot more often than not, smiling as I shoot teenagers on the paintball field, and outshooting most men on the gun range. I was and still am a tom boy at heart, dressed up in my mother's heels.

Within the workings of this home, the dominant belief system was that men worked outside the home, so women did all of the work inside the home. Since my mother worked as a beautician and worked 12-14 hrs. a day, by age eight I was responsible for all of the cleaning. Any of you have guys in the house? That's 5 guys without any accountability; a total get out of housework free card. It was a disgusting, perpetual mess!

I also did all of the cooking without the benefit of one single fast food restaurant or microwave oven, and in those days we made just a little extra so we could have leftovers the next day. Basically I made a meat and three, bread and dessert for 15 people at every meal I cooked. I am just thankful to God that he gave me the ability and desire because I love to cook.

It makes me happy to bring happiness through cooking, and anyone invited to my home knows the rules. First, the hostess prefers to go barefoot. Second, if you are hungry, I would love to cook for you.

I was also the primary caregiver for my one older stepbrother, younger brother, and two baby half brothers. As they arrived, each newborn would move into my room at six weeks old, and I would be in charge of getting them to sleep, respond to their cries in the middle of the night, and get up before school early enough to feed them before leaving for the day. Before I was a teenager, I had no idea who sung the latest songs on the radio, but I knew what colic was and the best ways to treat it. I taught them all to walk, talk, feed and dress themselves, and I would defend to blows anyone who picked on my boys. I would like to say I was a saint and enjoyed the responsibility. No, I did not perform these tasks grateful for the experience. I was young and rebellious and felt imprisoned. I wanted an escape.

My escape, my refuge was going to church. Obviously I was not attending with the best of intentions, but Oh how good God is and can use any circumstance for His glory! My family had never gone to church, prayed, or even opened the Bible that sat on the coffee table, and in the years that followed I can count on one hand their attendance, but they did allow me to go if I could get my own ride there. The sweetest Sunday school teacher in the world arranged for the church of a nearby town to send their bus out to collect me every Sunday morning. I would set my alarm, get myself ready, and be out the door to catch that bus all by myself. Sometimes I would be the only one on that bus, but I would be there, smiling and excited. Having a daughter that is eight years old at the time I am writing this story, I would never expect her to be so grown up and leave our house alone, church or not. It fills me with such wondrous awe in the sweet love and divine hand of my heavenly Father that He was at work in my life even before I knew Him.

So, at age 8 and all alone, I headed out to church. I can still see that green felt board Ms. Booth used to teach the Bible stories and remember her hand motions to the song "Deep and Wide". After kids church, we were permitted go to the main sanctuary for the message as long as we were seen and not heard. This church was tiny and poor in the eyes of the world, with only a few hard wooden pews and one stained glass window, but it had a Pastor as big around the middle as he was tall, who's heart overflowed with joy and love for the Lord.

Songs were sung by the choir only and there was no participation by the congregation, no clapping, no lifting of hands, just reverence-like to sing off key was an offense to God. To this day as I openly worship my Lord, horribly off key, I remember the restrictive atmosphere of the church of my youth and laugh with arms open at the freedom I now have. However, my God can work in any circumstance. One spring day as I was listening to the sermon, I felt a drawing as the Pastor asked if anyone wanted to accept Jesus as their Savior. I recall the sheer terror of those first two steps. Then, I think I ran down that aisle into his arms, crying and laughing, and wondering what in the world I had been scared of. Jesus wanted me!

God had called those ordinary people to teach and preach, and they were obedient, each doing the work God had called them to do. Their choice of obedience made a difference in my life. Jesus came and saved me at just the right time. He knew what was to come.

Only three short years later the dynamic of the household increased in wickedness. My stepfather and mother parents suffered seasons of serious illness or injury and money was nonexistent, so screaming and fights were an hourly occurrence. To complicate tension, my blossoming adolescence got the attention of male family members, and I found myself in an almost daily war to protect myself. While my mother knew what was happening, she was too weak to help me, and checked out emotionally and left me all alone.

In retaliation for my strength to stand, given to me by my Jesus, I would receive beatings from my abuser for any minor infraction, bruised stripes too numerous to count, until blood flowed or until he got tired. I knew the anger was fueled by my resistance to the advances and not justification for anything this trouble free, honor student had done.

With multiple surgeries for my mother's illnesses, came her resulting addiction to pain medications and even more money problems for the family. Deception was welcomed in and given the best seat in the house. Drugs were her only focus and stealing or lying to get them, just part of their relationship. When the drugs became too expensive or difficult to obtain, there was always liquor. I would like to say that I spent this torturous childhood seeking God's will for my life and praying for those who were my enemies.

Not me. I choose my own path and did not seek God's direction. I threw myself in the opposite direction of God and into the arms of a teenage boy that had a home life even more horrible than I had. His family setting was one of alcoholism and extreme physical violence. He had often told me stories of family fights involving guns and vehicles being used to try and run over himself, his brother, and mother. Where I wanted my life to be completely different than from the house I grew up in, he choose to follow in his father's footsteps. Out of the frying pan and into the fire. Three months into the marriage, I knew I had made a horrible mistake that lead to almost 10 years of abuse and control unlike anything I could have ever dreamed possible.

What I recognized as insecurity and immaturity in the early months of marriage and assumed would pass, grew into a malignant cancer eating away any goodness or kindness he had shown during courtship. Each year brought me further and further into seclusion as all friendships were driven away and even phone calls or laughter with my mother or grandmother sparked cruel interrogation. In the early years, a few minutes of his displeasure were all I could handle, and I would quickly break down into tears.

Sadly, in later years of marriage, when I had become as familiar with his torture as I was my own reflection, it took greater and more intense violence to tear down my wall of protection as minutes would pass into hours. His favorite pastime, his pleasure was in intimidation, violence and the threat of greater violence so persistent no force could stop his addiction until it was fully satisfied. Each time my collapse, my brokenness was his primary goal, not correcting any sin on my part, just my complete physical and spiritual defeat. After he was through, he would smile, an evil, self serving smile, and would then be ready to offer his forgiveness for whatever I had done wrong, and would remind me that he loved me. I Corinthians 13:4-6 says *"Love is patient and kind. Love is not jealous or boastful or proud or rude.*

It does not demand its own way. It is not irritable, and it keeps no record of being wronged. It does not rejoice about injustice but rejoices whenever the truth wins out".

I knew there was no love in my childhood home and I knew there was no love here, but I rationalized, I had made my choice. What difference did it make if I stayed with him or not? Families were not about fairy tale love and unity. They were dark and ugly, breaking you down and tearing at your soul until even the simple act of smiling was forbidden and foreign.

Then a miracle happened, he lost his job and we moved into a basement apartment with my grandmother, so I could be the primary breadwinner. A few years later the shock of my life, God allowed me to become pregnant. As my tummy grew, so did my love for that child. I read every book, took every class, never did an unhealthy food pass by my lips. My grandmother and I planned and shopped shamelessly, digging through sales tables at Dillard because this child "needed" a dozen sets of color coordinated sheets. I was neurotic and joyfully happy.

At the very beginning of my pregnancy when he attempted to continue his abusive behavior, some protective maternal instinct took over, and I challenged him for the first time in almost a decade. It was not right to attack a pregnant woman. Even he had some sense of conscious, and for nine peaceful months, I was left to nest and prepare.

With the birth of my daughter, I was overwhelmed at how my heart opened as I glanced into her perfect face. I say perfect, simply because she was. Her perfect C section head, little cherub face, dark brown eyes, flawless skin, kissable lips. I was protector of this baby. Every food she ate, outfit she wore, every decision was mine. Wow! What a responsibility. I had been blessed with a glimpse of just how much God really did love me, and as I fell in love with her I fell in love with my Savior all over again. I saw what love really was supposed to look like; light and fresh, hopeful and strong, enduring forever, all wrapped up in a bundle that smelled like Johnson's and Johnson' baby lotion. The thought of this child's death brought me to sobbing tears, and I knew I would die to protect her. More than that, God had sent His child to die for me, before I ever knew Him, He had died for ME. My heart grew so large at the first real physical understanding of how my God loved me.

In the months that followed, my sweet girl and I were inseparable. She had a smile that filled her face and insatiable appetite for books. We read, my grandmother read, and at nine months old, she said her first word: ambulance. Second word: mama. Third: May I have more please? I am not joking. She spoke two words and then jumped into full sentences! We would laugh together saying, she hasn't stopped talking since!

At his demand, we spent the first 18 weeks of her life sleeping on the living room couch so he would not be disturbed with her crying. He spoke of loving her but at the same time kept an unusual distance from her. Most days a kiss on her cheek was their only interaction before he would retreat to a television show. Some days he would never even see her. It was as if she was a possession, and not a favored one, to be taken out occasionally and then forgotten. I felt her rejection and ached for her. She too would grow up without a loving father.

My anger increased rapidly in the following months. Still too fearful of physical harm, I instead lashed out at him with my actions, making bad decision after bad decision in my anger; fueling his temper in hopes that he would leave us. One evening while he was holding the baby we began to fight and he did the unimaginable. In a fit of rage, he took my 15 month old daughter and threw her across the room toward me, trying to hurt me by hurting her. Praise God I was able to move fast enough to catch her before she struck the ground. I looked into his face distorted with rage and, no longer caring how much punishment I had to endure, I told him to leave. He destroyed the apartment and everything in it in his rage, but mindful that he was living in my grandmother's home, left without harming me or the baby.

I knew that I had not been a biblical wife, loving and respecting, showing Christ before my husband and being submissive and prayerful over the marriage. I knew that God did not like divorce, but I also knew that He did not want me and my child spending the rest of our lives living in terror. Examining my past and realizing it would be her future, I had to do what my mother had been incapable of doing for me. I had to save my daughter. With the same fear filled steps that took me down the aisle to salvation years before, I walked into a law-yer's office and had divorce paperwork signed by the end of business hours the next day.

My heart was broken, not for the failed marriage, but that even as I was escaping my boogeyman, my daughter was ordered by the court to continue visitation. Failure in trying to run my own life bled into my daughter's life, and it was with that realization that I hum-bly began my journey back to God, asking for and receiving complete forgiveness for my contribution to our failed marriage. I was so far from the little girl of eight, but I was still His and He was ready to lovingly receive me. God gave me so much more than I ever imagined or deserved.

I was introduced to an incredible man, a young entrepreneur in town, four years my junior but an old soul. The moment I looked into his beautiful blue eyes, my heart awakened and the Holy Spirit whis-per, "this one". He was captivating, mischievous, intelligent, funny, and a hard worker. We spent numerous weeks talking on the phone for hours at a time before I consented to meet for a date, asking each other every question, learning every detail of our personalities. We fell completely and totally in love over the phone.

I had found the man God had set up for me, and we laughed, although sadly, when we realized that we were traveling in the same circles, with the same friends just prior to my first marriage. Had I only sought God instead of my own plan for my life, I would not have married my first husband. My daughter knows that she is an incred-ible blessing. She was God's wake up call to my heart, and that I could not imagine life without her, but she also knows my impatience to wait on God's perfect plan caused me a 10 year season of misery which bled over into her life.

Our courtship was a whirlwind of new experiences and filled with laughter, and a few months after our introduction, I found myself on an island with my best friend and a Pastor waiting on me to walk down the path to my second wedding. This time would be different. As I paced back and forth, I earnestly prayed to God for wisdom. He would tell me "this one" and I would remind him that we had only met a few months before. Then he would say again, "this one". Finally I gave up trying to argue and walked out of the room in obedience.

I would like to say I was instantly healed, but I wasn't. I was constantly asking my husband if he was going to leave and compared him to the other men who had hurt me in the past. I was so insecure, but he responded with gentleness and understanding. He was in love and was not going anywhere. Plagued with nightmares for several years, I would wake shaking and crying and each time he held me, somehow knowing exactly what I needed, even to the point of sleeping in a closet without windows when I was too scared to sleep in an open room. He was encouraging when I needed encouragement and was protective when I was fragile.

After such a difficult childhood and first marriage, my new life was almost too good to be true. A business birthed by God alone and three more children later, I finally had my family I had always dreamed of and there was nothing more important to me. I was going to hold onto this life, this family with all I had. Nothing would come between us or tear us apart. Then ten years after saying "I do" on that island came that letter telling me to prepare to die.

I was overwhelmed and crushed. I collapsed to the floor in a heap and cried out to God "WHY? What am I to learn through this"? He has carried me through my childhood, my first marriage, and now this? My heart reached out to Him and He reminded me He works everything to the good for those who believe in Him. I calmed down and began to pray.

In the days that followed the letter, several tests were performed by my doctors and all turned out to be false, I did not have HIV. I was not going to die from that disease; however, I do not believe receipt of that letter had no purpose. God was calling me. It was time to dig deeper. I began to closely evaluate my life, and to determine if I was living in a way pleasing to God. Would I be welcomed into the Kingdom of heaven, greeted as a good and faithful servant when it was my time to die? Wiggling in my chair, I didn't think so.

As I prayed, the Lord reminded me of a sermon I had recently heard about dying to self and following Him. Dying, how appropriate. But, wasn't I doing that? I went to church every Sunday, volunteered anywhere there was a need, and took women's Bible Study classes from time to time. Wasn't I doing well enough?

My Lord led me to Luke 9:23-24 which says *"If any of you wants to be my follower, you must turn from your selfish ways, take up your cross daily, and follow me. If you try to hang on to your life, you will lose it. But if you give up your life for my sake, you will save it"*. I thought to myself.... Am I selfish? I put my family first above all else. I love them more than anything. I'm always putting them before me. Who more than God knew from what I had survived! What more could I give?

He then took me to Matthew 10:37 which says "If you love your father or mother more than you love me, you are not worthy of being mine; or if you love your son or daughter more than me, you are not worthy of being mine.

There it was. Ten years with my first husband, ten years with my second. This was no coincidence! He wanted to be number one in my life in bad times and in good times. I neglected to praise Him through my pain, but I had also neglected to praise him through my blessings. The Holy Spirit got face to face with me and revealed to me Abba Father was the only Father I had ever known, and yet I so easily replaced him with my desires, my agenda. I put my most important relationship at the bottom of the list after husband, children, work, volunteering, household chores, and afternoon naps. I allowed no time for Him with everything I had to get done each day; after all, I had a busy family of six and growing business. How ungrateful I was! After that He had brought me out of 28 years of suffering, this was how I repaid Him? I got so distracted living *"my"* life and I forgot that I am His and He is mine! Our relationship should have come before any other. I was sick of myself. I cried out to Him to forgive me and help me. No fancy prayer, just...*"help me, I am nothing without you"*.

Then my truly amazing, merciful, loving Father said "My Child, get up!" "I picked you up and kept you going during the abandonment of your father, the abuse by your stepfather, the neglect and emotional abuse of your drug and alcohol addicted mother, I protected and strengthened you during your first marriage, I delivered your firstborn from the hands of wickedness, and I will pick you up now". Oh, praise God for His goodness and grace!

He led me to Luke 8:54 which says, *"Then Jesus took her by the hand and said in a loud voice, "My child, get up!"* And at that moment her life returned, and she immediately stood up! Jesus was speaking in Luke about resurrecting a child from death, but that is exactly what He did for my life. With sweet gentleness and love, He took my hand and lifted me up, teaching me that in putting down *"my"* life and setting my eyes on Him, I would build my life on a foundation that can never fail. He is always trustworthy, always perfect, and He loves me and you so much. Oh how He longs to do the same for you if you will only trust Him and ask!

I opened my full heart to Him, trusting and not expecting to be punished but to be accepted and loved as a daughter of the King of Kings. Diving into His word, praying for wisdom and understanding, bowing in submission to His will and authority over my life, I found my life. It is in my relationship with Jesus Christ, with Him as first place in my life.

I know I am an unfinished work of art, but the closer I become to Him, the sooner I realize when I am stepping out of His light, and the faster I am to repent and to ask for His forgiveness. I know what He will say whenever I do... *"My Child, get up"*.

Redemption: I Choose Life

By Kristin Jordan

This story begins on one of the toughest days of my life. I spent most of the day at the hospital because of a skin condition that looked like bee stings all over my legs, arms, and torso. The doctors who looked at me grimaced at the sight and told me that I had everything from Syphilis to Gonorrhea. As I waited for the final test results there was a constant battle going on within my mind.

Just days before I entered the hospital emergency room, I found out that my husband had been unfaithful throughout our entire marriage. I was devastated thinking that everything we had lived through together for the past six years had all been a BIG lie! Not only did I find out that there had been many women in his life, but two of them were my *"friends"*. Everyone knew except me and I felt betrayed on the highest level.

The physical deformity of my body was nothing compared to the way I felt on the inside. *How did this happen? How had I gotten to the point of wanting to end it all?*

As I sat in the hospital, I remembered the first time I felt so broken, betrayed and abandoned. It was when I was four years old when my mom had confronted my dad about his affair with a co-worker. After all the hollering and fighting, he was leaving... leaving for good! Although the memory was years past, it was still so vivid and real that I could recall every smell, sound, and word spoken. I watched him leave, not looking back only to remember the deep and intense hurt within my heart.

My father was my rock and when he left, I was so broken that I built a fortress around my heart that set the wheels in motion for a series of destructive choices and cycles in my life to come.

My parents had both married and divorced several times. The constant revolving door of destructive and abusive relationships had left me with low self esteem, insecurity, physical and mental abuse, alcoholism, drug addictions, molestation, fear, and the need for others' approval. I was constantly searching for ways to numb the pain and escape my reality.

My only saving grace had been my grandfather who loved me and treated me like an absolute princess. He encouraged me to pursue the greatness that lived inside of me and had quickly taken my father's place filling the void in my life. But as life would have it, things took another twisted turn. My grandfather was diagnosed with bone cancer and was only given a few months to live. *How could that be?* I had wondered. *Why would God take my only advocate? With all of the worthless people in the world, why would He take the only one who loved me?*

My grandfather had outlived the diagnosis by almost four years, but eventually he had succumbed to the deadly disease. I was thirteen when he died, and once again felt devastated, abandoned and rejected.

Now I was mad! I was mad at God, my Mom and the world and began to act out and rebel. I purposely hung out with the wrong crowd and began to steal, lie, cut school, drink, fight, and cuss. I became mentally and verbally abusive to my Mom and wanted her to feel my pain while looking for love and acceptance anywhere I could find it. I was a time bomb just waiting to explode.

On my destructive path, I met a dancer that introduced me to a community center where they taught performing arts which became my safe place of refuge. I studied stage management and learned how to dance, rap, sing and write. This is where I fell in love with another dancer and dated for most of my high school years.

My Mom hated the center, my boyfriend and me. And honestly, she had every right because I was so disrespectful and mean spirited.

I finally began to clean up my act and got involved in sports and the student counsel. I tried to stay out of trouble, but whenever I tried to do what was right, evil was always present.

Eventually, I realized what seemed to be perfect was not so perfect. I noticed my boyfriend began doing odd things, and after weeks of observation, I found that he was cheating on me with a so-called "friend."

As I sat at the hospital recalling that relationship, it hit me like a ton of bricks! I was caught in a cycle! Sixteen years later and I was still wrestling that same demon. *"That should tell me something about my friend selection,"* I said under my breath. I thought so much had changed, but really, the script was the same ... the only difference was the cast.

Reflecting on the cycle, I thought about another chapter in my life when I had received several college scholarships and went to play basketball at Sonoma State University. I had moved out with some friends who played for the SSU Men's Basketball Team, and the star player kept asking me out. At first I wasn't interested, but the more I denied him, the more he pursued. Finally, I gave in and fell in love. His ex-girlfriend started showing up only to find out that he had been seeing her behind my back. When I confronted him, he lied and I believed him. The confrontation ended with a brutal fight with the girl, being beaten up by my boyfriend, and almost having a near death experience because of it.

That day in the hospital lobby, I realized I was in the same cycle only at an escalated level! Until then, I had never thought about those chapters in my life in the context of one feeding off of another. *Had this pattern been going on my whole life? Can I have any man or friend in my life that I can trust?* The longer I sat there, the more depressed I became.

Shortly thereafter, I moved to LA to attend California State University Fulton to study Business Administration. I moved into an apartment complex with some friends and we met some guys who were part of the Phi Beta Sigma fraternity and began dating one of them.

After school started, I decided I wanted to join a sorority, so I went to rush night at the sister sorority, Zeta Phi Beta. After deciding I wanted to join, I found out the guy I had been dating was one of my big sister's ex-boyfriends. She made my life a living hell and tried to make sure I didn't get into the sorority. In order to punish me, she "dropped dime," or told on our line, and we were suspended. It took us over a year to finally gain acceptance to the sorority, but only after total heartbreak and chaos. Only two out of four girls were allowed to "cross." All over a boy! And ironically, throughout our pledge process, the guy was sleeping with his ex-girlfriend again. Once again, I felt betrayed by both of them.

I thought back to when I had first met my husband. I had been at the Alpha Kappa Ball with my best friend and my future husband had danced his way into my heart. After our first date we were inseparable. He was my soul mate; I was sure of it.

For three months, we got lost in each other; then one afternoon while at his mother's house looking through photo albums at his graduation pictures, I got side-swiped with another dagger. The girl standing in the picture with him was a member of my sorority house ... one of my friends. What a disaster! For this, there would be more hell to pay in my sorority.

When my sorority sisters found out, they gave me an ultimatum: either leave my boyfriend, or they would black ball me out of the sorority. My disdain for girls grew exponentially that day. How crazy was that? Choose the sisterhood or him? I choose him!

Then things began to change, he was let go from his job and fell into a deep depression. After weeks of trying to get him motivated to get off the couch and out of the dark, I made a decision to leave. During this separation I dedicated my life to my Lord and Savior Jesus Christ and this was a huge turning point because I was committed to live right while seeking God's will for my life.

During that time, my boyfriend got himself back together and begged me to come back to him. I told him everything had changed; that it wouldn't be the same. I laid the foundation of my new life by telling him, *"no more living together without being married, no more sex, and no more fornication."* WHAT? I explained to him, *"If that doesn't work for you, there is no future for us."*

Although he didn't want to agree to "no sex until we are married relationship", he agreed and we got back together. Just because things had changed in my mind didn't mean his "desires" had changed. While I waited for him in his room one day, I found a condom wrapper in his bed. Since we weren't having sex, there was only one conclusion and that conclusion was that he was having sex with someone and that someone was not me!

I confronted him immediately and he confessed. He begged for forgiveness, but I ran out in hysterics. I was once again betrayed and devastated.

I committed myself deeper into the church and tuned out the world. He tried to call me, would cry on the phone to my mom, and just would not leave me alone. Night after night it was the same routine. He would fall asleep on my porch, and I would pray, *"Please God, get this man away from me. If he is not for me, get him away from me"*. But the more I prayed, the more he pursued.

As I sat in the hospital that day, about to tear my skin off because of the lesions, I began to doubt my faith, my God, and my choices. I questioned whether I had really heard from God or had perhaps heard the enemy and not been able to identify him.

I thought back to the months and months of pleading and begging. I had told my boyfriend he had to get in church and accept Christ as his Savior before I would even consider talking to him, and he did. Not only had he gone to church, he had jumped in with both feet. The more spiritual he became, the more forgiveness seeped into my heart and the more attractive he became.

I tried to pray him away, but the more I tried, the closer we grew. Finally, on Valentine's Day, he proposed, and I accepted. I thought all of the foolishness was behind us. I also believed that since we were spiritually on the right track our marriage was destined for success without any speed bumps.

During the first year of our marriage we pursued our dream of music and prepared an album. In early 1995, our album was released and exploded to the top of the charts as the #1 record in the country.

While managing my husband, I became extremely focused on my career and was eager to make my mark in the music business. We immediately went from barely making any money to having multi-millions. The problem however, was that I was focused on my husband's career, not his "needs." I was completely oblivious to what was really going on around me, and that left the door wide open for the enemy through a flood of girls to rush in on our marriage.

Three days before entering the hospital doors, all those years of marriage came to a crashing halt. It was almost my birthday, and my best friend, Montell, and I were scheduled to go out of town to celebrate. She called the day before we were to go and told me she was not going. Then she asked if Montell was there.

I immediately hit her with questions: *"Why? What do you mean? What's wrong?"* She seemed very upset; I had never heard her like that. *"Was it something I did?"* I asked. She said, *"No, but where is Montell?"* I said, *"Right here"* then handed him the phone.

She spoke to him for about five minutes, and when he got off the phone, his eyes were panic stricken. I asked him what was wrong, and he said, *"I have something to tell you."* Then he confessed his indiscretions and infidelities. It was about 30 minutes of verbal vomit that seemed to last an eternity. I was in shock and disbelief for about the first 15 minutes, and then anger set in. As he detailed his escapades, I made him name names and give details. I was furious and called him everything but a child of God. *How could he have done that to me?*

I was called back into reality by a nurse calling, my name. I went in to see the doctor and for about an hour they ran an arsenal of tests. The results were inconclusive, so they gave me a few prescriptions for the itching and pain and diagnosed me with extreme stress.

As I drove back to the house, I was hysterical and wanted to just run off the road into a ditch. I sobbed most of the night and at the break of dawn I decided that I had enough. I ran outside, hopped in my truck, and took off driving like a bat out of hell. I drove down a dark, windy back road and pulled into a church parking lot. I recognized I had a problem bigger than myself and that one of two things was going to happen. I was either going to drive my truck off a cliff, or I was going to go inside the church and throw myself on the altar. I chose the altar.

I went into the house of God, threw myself on the altar, and cried out to God like never before. I knew I didn't want to go back or go on, but instead of submitting to my will, I did what I had avoided doing all week. I said, *"God, what do you want me to do?"* Of course, you can imagine what He said ... the unthinkable. He said, *"STAY!"*

After much crying out, soul searching, repentance, and sorrow, I chose to forgive, and STAY. That was not the choice my flesh wanted to make. I had wanted to run; but God told me that my future and my child's future depended on me staying.

Over time and with the grace of God, it got better. My heart healed, our marriage healed, and we began to rebuild our lives. God took us through a wilderness experience that would have killed most, but we survived.

My husband and I have fought the good fight, and we are now happily married. I know now that HE was the man I was dreaming of all along. That's what God can do. God took everything the enemy was trying to kill and turned it around so we could use it for God's glory. God has truly restored us.

I am now speaking and leading in the Recycled Women Ministry and my husband and I also have a marriage ministry called Marriage MasterPeace. Through the marriage ministry; we teach couples how to communicate, prioritize, and wade through the tough issues.

Who would have guessed that through all that pain and mess I would find a great marriage with unspeakable joy, a peace that surpasses all understanding, and be able to find the gift that God has given me to use to help others. My God is a redeemer, a restorer, and a deliverer that in Him ALL things are possible.

.

A New Beginning

By Ouida Guinn

Believing you are *more* important than you are, or believing you are *less* important than you are can both be dangerous. Yet the Holy Spirit can build upon an open heart, whoever we are, to increase God's kingdom. Thus I share with you my story of God's powerful work for my good and His glory.

As a youth I excelled athletically and socially. Yet academics, and especially reading, were so burdensome for me that I learned to hate school. Even with extra help I could not conquer the all-important language arts hurdles. I even tried college, but dropped out in discouragement. Only later in adulthood was I diagnosed with dyslexia. In most other ways my life was typical and traditional for the times (40s and 50s). Mom was at home while Dad worked long hours. My younger brother lived to aggravate me. Dinner was served around the table where the day's events were discussed. With no television we had favorite radio shows. There were sock-hops at school but I never encountered drinking, drugs or sex, even though some of that may have been back in the shadows. My life was a lot like "Happy Days."

Being well protected, naive and shy, when a handsome, flamboyant young man came into my life I was totally swept off my feet. Different than any guy I'd ever known, his bold presence filled the room when he walked in. Although I rebuffed his quick talk of marriage, it happened ten short months later. Three months after that I found I was pregnant. I was making another discovery, too. This charming man was an alcoholic. The joy of welcoming a son into our family was soured by drinking episodes that left me afraid and confused. This is not how I pictured family life. Money was scarce, my husband was angry a lot — and I felt trapped. I had unwittingly made him my god and he was deeply disappointing me.

Not every day was terrible, but many were. There were enough decent times for me to feel I could 'hang in there.' I just knew things would change if I was a good enough wife. My husband traveled a lot with his work, but most of the time when he was home, he drank and was angry. Looking back, I think he was scared.

My second pregnancy produced a beautiful girl. In spite of that blessing I was living in a hell at 25 years of age. With two children and an abusive, jealous husband, I had little education and was totally discouraged from working outside the home. Hating who I had become, I cried out to God, *"What am I going to do?"*

Time went on. There were occasions when I could see my husband doing his best to love us. Yet his addictions and my trapped feelings clashed to bring out the worst in both of us. What I did have was my children — and I poured myself into them. But once again, time kept moving and the day came when they were out on their own. Now I was really lost. I thought, *"God, now what do I do?"* Finally, after 40 years of marriage, I mustered up the nerve to ask for a divorce. Our mutual opposition to one another bumped up to a whole new level.

My husband wasn't given to losing and he did his best to make the process of divorce as painful as possible for me. He promised to drag me through every possible court, accusing me of unfaithfulness and every other unworthiness of getting any benefits from him. He was relentless. Some of my friends were afraid for my life.

The end of this finally came when in my utter misery I knew I could not handle the pressure and personal attacks any longer. My resolution to this was to take myself out of the situation by ending my life. After writing letters to my children and grandchildren I drove to the bank where I kept a firearm in a lockbox — my weapon of self-destruction. Unbelievably, the bank was closed. It was Saturday. My shock and disbelief turned to rage and hopelessness. I remained isolated the rest of the day at home alone. A phone call from a friend allowed me to turn the corner.

My friend advised me of hard information that my husband had not been faithful to me through the years. When I faced him with these facts over the phone, his silence confirmed the truth. Suddenly, with the power of truth on my side, the harassing stopped and the divorce was finalized soon after with little additional fanfare. In hindsight I clearly see God's hand in protecting me from self-destruction and in sending a friend with clarifying facts that moved a muddy divorce to completion.

Later on, I started dating a precious man. He was quiet, unassuming, supportive, funny, and kind in every way. He was a precious Christian man, and he made me feel safe. I have to say, it took a few years before I felt completely safe. We have been dating almost 10 years now, and we do seem to bring out the best in each other.

As life moved on, I'll have to say that I took several trips to that 'Forgiveness Cross' before I was finally able to lay down my unforgiveness and not pick it back up. Forgiveness is now the biggest blessing in my life. Does that mean I have forgotten what happened in my life? No, but, I have forgiven what happened to me and have recognized my ownership in what took place. I have also forgiven myself.

Four years ago in the early spring, my ex-husband was diagnosed with lung cancer. By then we had each experienced the redemption and forgiveness of God through Jesus Christ. Due to that forgiveness in my life, I was able to compassionately help with his care and rebuild a friendship relationship with him right up until he passed into eternity. My new friend was most supportive of my taking this role.

I have told you this story so you could see just how lost I was and how, with God's help, I came to value life. Today, I choose to have a Christian environment. I know God will "cover me with His feathers," and "under His wings I will find refuge."

I firmly believe that God "rearranged" the players in my life in just such a way that His will could be accomplished. God's plan is so much better than ours. That's why the bank was closed that Saturday morning long ago. In His mercy He turned the terrible black cloud of my life into many avenues of blessing.

It is inevitable that life on earth encounters trials and tribulations along with times of joy. Christ did not promise total ease and relaxation; He did promise that we could become new creations in Him. If fact, He tells us that bad times will come. They are actually important times in our lives that, if endured with Christ leading the way, help grow us in faith and perseverance.

As we continually reorder our lives through our relationships with Jesus Christ and spend time in God's Word, He will reveal His will to us and help us grow and mature. I now love my life and know that with God, all things are possible!

The God Who Laughed at My Jokes

By Laurette Willis

When I was a little girl growing up in the suburbs of Long Island, I felt very close to God—and it wasn't the God I experienced in the church we attended. That God seemed rather distant and stuffy.

My mother enjoyed telling the story of what happened the first time we went to St. Thomas Episcopal Church when I was three years old. As we sat in the crowded sanctuary that hot and humid Sunday morning I screamed, *"Get me out of here!"*

In time, I became accustomed to the church. I memorized the prayers and knew exactly when we were supposed to kneel, cross ourselves and answer in unison. I could mimic Father Palmer's British accent when he said that Jesus is "our only mediator and advocate." I didn't know what it meant, but I liked the way he said it. I did my best to imitate his round vowels under my breath, until my mother would tell me to stop.

How different that was from my experiences with God in my room. I had an illustrated children's Bible and enjoyed telling my stuffed animals the stories by looking at the pictures before I could read the words. I would place them in a semi-circle around me, show them the pictures, and act out the stories using a variety of different accents and animal sounds. I enjoyed seeing how many voices and characters I could create. This ability with dialects came in handy later in years as an actor, storyteller and comedienne Off-Broadway known as *"The Woman of 101 Voices."*

I did my best to come up with a punch line at the end of each Bible story to make God laugh. I figured He had such a hard job that He needed a good chuckle now and then.

"So God said to Noah," I told my captive audience. "'Noah, build Me an ark!' And Noah said, 'Okay, God. That's right up my alley!'" As an aside, I added, "Won't God get a kick out of that?" And I believed He absolutely did!

During the account of Daniel in the lions' den when God spared Daniel's life by closing the lions' mouths, I suggested the head lion mumbled, "No lunch today, boys." When David hurled the stone at the giant Goliath's head, it landed "smack-dab in the middle of his forehead—and you know that hurt like the Dickens," I added.

Hearing God's Voice in My Closet

As a small child, whenever someone hurt my feelings I ran home crying and hid in my bedroom closet. If Robbie said I was fat, or Willie pushed me in my little red bathing suit into the bramble bushes, or Karen didn't want to play with me, it was hard to hold back the tears. I'd run home as fast as I could. The moment the closet door was shut, I was safe. Sitting on a pile of shoes and toys, hidden among the shirts and dresses, no one could hurt me.

For three years God met me in that closet. Tears streaming down my face, I shut the door and sat in the comforting darkness. After a few moments I saw a flash of light. A bright scene appeared on the inside of the closet door as if it were a movie screen. In this open-eyed vision I stood behind a curtain and watched an adult version of myself onstage in front of a vast outdoor audience. The grown-up Laurette had one hand lifted high above her head and appeared to be speaking or singing into a microphone in the other hand. In front of me were thousands of people who also had their hands lifted toward the sky.

I instinctively knew the people were worshiping God, even though I'd never witnessed such behavior at St. Thomas Episcopal Church. The only time I'd seen people's hands go above waist-level was to hold a hymnal. Years later I learned that was a common way to worship God in ancient Israel and the early Christian church.

After a few seconds the vision faded and I heard a comforting voice over my right shoulder. "Everything is going to be all right," He said. In my heart, I knew this was God's voice. His voice hugged me and gave me peace. "Everything's gonna be all right," I repeated after Him, sniffling and wiping my tears on my sleeve. Standing up, I opened the door and stepped out of the closet to face the world again.

This happened many times over a three-year period between the ages of three and six. Nothing seemed unusual about these encounters, probably because I had nothing with which to compare them. Whenever I was upset, I knew I could run into my closet and hide from the world, but not from God. He met me there and comforted me. He always understood, showed me what I believed was a vision of my future, and assured me everything was going to be all right. I could trust Him. He would never hurt or disappoint me.

The Wall Around Me

When I was six years old, something changed. I no longer felt that closeness with the Lord. The only way I could describe it was to say it felt like there was a thick wall around me, separating me, protecting me from everyone and everything. I felt safe inside this walled fortress, but I also felt empty and alone—except when Mommy and I would play.

We'd giggle like girlfriends as we took long walks through the neighborhood holding hands. Acting out all the characters to the *Peter Pan* album I got for Christmas, we'd fly around the playroom singing "I won't grow up!" Snuggling together on the couch we read *Little Women* aloud with English accents...

My beautiful mother Jacqueline was a petite, blue-eyed strawberry-blonde. She was brilliant and funny with a voice like warm honey; an Irish colleen who spoke fluent Spanish and enjoyed parsing words back to their Latin origins. A frustrated actor and singer, she was an attorney and the first woman Assistant District Attorney on Long Island. She later became one of only two female Assistant District Attorneys out of over 130 A.D.A.s in District Attorney Frank Hogan's office in New York City. I was so proud of her.

Although I could never believe it, I loved when people said, *"You're just like your mother."* She was stunning. I felt ugly. Sadly, this remarkable woman with the movie star good looks, brilliant mind and tender heart became an alcoholic who had three nervous breakdowns and attempted suicide when I was a child.

Things looked so perfect on the outside of our beautiful home on Long Island, but behind closed doors were pain, torment and tears.

To comfort myself, I developed an unhealthy attachment to food. I remember running into my parents' bedroom and kneeling beside the bed. On a bright, beautiful mid-afternoon in suburban Long Island, Mommy was asleep in her darkened bedroom. Was she depressed, or had she been drinking?

I was small, a little pudgy, with dimpled hands and knees, my round "Campbell kids" face framed with a brunette pixie cut. Tears pooled in bright amber eyes and flowed down chubby little cheeks as I patted Mommy's face.

"Mommy! Mommy!" I cried. *"I can't stop eating."*

For the past hour the little girl her mother called *"Little Laurie So-Sweet"* had been eating bread and butter, Easy-Bake Oven cake mix, cereal and anything else I could find to comfort me while Mommy slept. I was six years old and food was my friend.

At Northside Elementary School when the boys discovered I'd cry when they called me "Fatso," it became a favorite taunt. I remember many days running home from school in tears. An only child, I was unaccustomed to the teasing children often do. I didn't understand why they were so mean to me.

"I know what they're really saying," I'd tell my mother. *"They're saying I have a 'fat soul,' huh Mommy?"* It was a silly thing to say. I knew it wasn't true. I was just trying to ease the tension for both of us.

Once alone in my room I'd look in the mirror and scold myself, *"You're fat! You're ugly! You're stupid! I hate you!"* Then came the tears. After the tears came the search for food. I'd watch television and eat until I was numb. It was an unending cycle that continued for over thirty years.

I attempted my first diet when I was eleven years old. I saved up the money from my lemonade stand and secretly went into the neighborhood drug store to buy a box of *amazing* weight loss candies.

"These are for your mother, right?" the pharmacist asked, peering over his spectacles.

"Uh, yes," I lied.

One weight loss candy was to be eaten with a glass of water in place of a meal or for a snack. I ate half the box at one sitting and hid the rest under my dresser. They were delicious. I gained three pounds.

It's surprising that I didn't become heavier than I did. I attribute this to my mother becoming the town's first "health-food nut," as people interested in nutrition were called in the 1960s. When Mom was following a healthy diet, taking vitamins and exercising daily she didn't drink alcohol as much—sometimes not at all which was marvelous to me.

While other children's lunchboxes had Twinkies and Yodels with their bologna sandwiches on white bread, I had celery sticks and apple slices with my tuna sandwich on whole grain bread. I didn't seem to mind the kids' taunts about the weird food. I made it a game. I could eat carrot sticks like a rabbit and do an impression of Bugs Bunny to make them laugh. Ah—an audience! I loved it.

Over the next twenty-plus years, food was my primary *"drug of choice."* If I ate enough of it, it numbed me. Food, and later alcohol, cigarettes, drugs, reckless relationships and New Age spiritual practices were some of the things I used to fill the missing piece on the inside of me since *"the wall"* went up—the wall which separated me from God.

Numbness, I discovered, is a poor substitute for peace.

The Little Yogini

When I was seven years old my mother became involved in yoga. A nice-looking Asian couple had a popular daytime yoga program on television. It was scheduled right after Jack LaLanne's exercise show. It seemed so harmless, so relaxing and so *spiritual*.

The exercises relaxed Mom. Being an only child, my mother and I did almost everything together. We did yoga exercises together too.

When she began teaching free yoga classes to high school and college students in our home, I was the little demonstration model. I loved the attention. My father thought it was all rather kooky, but he was busy building his law practice and didn't pay much attention to what we did when he wasn't home.

For several years Mom and I visited Ananda Ashram, a yoga retreat in upstate New York associated with Swami Satchidananda. When I was ten years old, the Swami visited the ashram while we were there and 'blessed' me. His smell was overpoweringly sweet. His long, wavy black hair was heavy with oil, and always looked wet as it flowed over his saffron shoulders. I suppose the attention was to make me feel *"special."* I just felt uncomfortable.

During meditation times, I wouldn't keep my eyes closed. I kept peeking at all the serene-looking adults in the room as we sat cross-legged in the lotus posture, incense filling the air. I liked doing the exercises better.

For 22 years I was an avid student of Hatha Yoga, and was an instructor for part of that time. I also practiced Kundalini yoga. During my late teens and 20s I studied a variety of spiritual practices, seeking to recover the God of my childhood, although I didn't realize it at the time. I knew something was missing. Everything I studied, every conference I attended, each book I read and course I took was an attempt to find the Lord who loved me and laughed at my jokes.

My studies included a variety of metaphysical philosophies and practices from A to Z: Astrology to Zoroastrianism; Kabbalah, Mystical Christianity, Hinduism, various types of yoga; shamanism, Tibetan Buddhism, Universal Mind, Hawaiian Huna; Urantia, Course in Miracles and writings from other channeled entities, spirit guides and Ascended Masters.

"I Feel Dead Inside"

In my 20s I lived in New York City and was the typical 'struggling actor.' I lived in the East Village and worked part-time as a secretary and waitress "to support my acting habit," as I put it. I fearfully went to auditions on my days off, but most of the time I drank white wine, watched television and read New Age books.

In March 1982 I visited my mother who was working as an attorney for the Thruway Authority in upstate New York. She and my stepfather Fred were separated and Mom was very depressed. We got drunk together. *"I feel dead inside,"* Mom said. I tried to encourage her with Tarot card readings and prompted her to get in touch with the light within, but nothing seemed to help. She said she felt as if she had no hope. There was a great sadness in her eyes. She looked lost.

A week later I got a call from Fred. My mother had aimed a .357 Magnum at her heart and pulled the trigger. She missed the first time, but the second attempt hit its mark. The first bullet lodged itself in the bedroom wall, prompting police investigators to consider her death was a homicide, but they later ruled it a suicide. I was grateful for that. As horribly painful as her death was, I couldn't stand the thought of someone else taking her life.

My boyfriend Damien and my stepfather tried to keep me out of the bedroom where Mom took her life. While they were out, I carefully wiped up her blood from the wooden floorboards and wall. I didn't want anyone else to do it. Crying, I held her hairbrush close to my face, closed my eyes and took a deep breath. Her scent was still there, but she was gone.

"You're just like your mother."

As the months passed, I drank more and went to fewer auditions. They scared me. Almost everything scared me or made me feel insecure. I walked along the streets with my eyes downcast. Talking to people frightened me, but it was easier after a few drinks.

Every so often I would hear a voice in my head say words that used to delight me, *"You're just like your mother."* Who said that? Where did those thoughts come from? Now those words tormented me.

A talent with character voices and dialects landed me a job with the First Amendment Comedy & Improvisation Company Off-Broadway where I was given the nickname *"The Woman of 101 Voices."* I did the one-woman performance *"The Betty Boop Show"* and appeared on television with the woman who did the original voices for Betty Boop and Popeye's Olive Oyl, Mae Questel. People said I was *"the funniest woman they had ever seen."*

While confident on-stage, I felt insecure off-stage. I continued on my search for inner peace and spiritual enlightenment. I practiced meditation, chanting, aura balancing, chakra cleansing, past life recall, psychism, and channeling. I visited shamans, psychics, sweat lodges, caves and shrines.

In addition to all these things, I studied bits and pieces from the Bible, but believed the Christian worldview was 'kindergarten' compared to the higher truths I imagined. I believed the answers I sought were just around the corner in the next conference, the next book, the next spiritual high. I was certain I was just one experience away from being the person I longed to be.

Before every new experience I felt hope and excitement. During each experience I felt closer than I had ever been before. I wanted a real, verifiable experience with God. "Maybe this is it!" I thought. But then afterwards I felt the let-down, and the emptiness returned. I felt like a donkey following a carrot dangling from a string placed in front of its nose. I continually sought the next spiritual experience, the next new teaching. Where was the God of my childhood?

You Can Always Return to Me

My mother had a little rhyme she would repeat from time-to-time when I was a child. As I sat on her lap, she'd hold me in her arms, gently rocking me and saying, *"Travel the whole world over. Sail the deep blue sea. When your wanderlust is over, you can always return to me."*

I wanted to travel the whole world over. I felt that if I were to visit some of the sacred sites I'd read about I would have a spiritual experience that would change me and I'd become the focused, confident, spiritually-enlightened person I longed to be.

In the mid-1980s my father became very ill with complications from heart disease and diabetes. I was grateful I could be with him in the hospital during the last weeks of his life. Even though Dad had not been to church in years, I learned that Father Palmer, who had been the priest at St. Thomas Episcopal Church, visited my father and prayed with him. That meant a lot to me, and I noticed that Dad was remarkably calmer the last week of his life. He didn't seem scared anymore or see fearsome apparitions. The man who could fly into a rage at the least provocation seemed peaceful for the first time in his life. It wasn't until years later that I realized what may have happened during Father Palmer's visit. Dad made his peace with God.

After Dad's passing, I was able to do the travel I'd wanted to do. I went to many of the world's sacred sites in Europe, the U.S. and Peru. I spent thousands of dollars and countless hours looking for God and searching for enlightenment. At one spiritual conference, I was suddenly lifted thirty feet in the air looking down at the top of everyone's head—although physically my feet never left the floor. I felt giddy and elated for about 20 seconds, and then it was over. At an event in California a famous channeled entity challenged me when I said I had a "tremendous desire to serve people." The supposed Ascended Master scolded me in front of 1200 followers, *"Serve thyself, entity!"* I felt hurt. My high hopes of being my own god were dashed. "I'm hopeless," I thought.

I visited Stonehenge and Glastonbury in England, in search of mystical encounters. One morning I rose before dawn and climbed Chalice Hill in Glastonbury, overlooking the site of mythical Avalon of Arthurian legend, supposed resting place of the Holy Grail. Standing alone beside St. Michael's Tower, I looked out over the fog-laden valley. I felt no closer to God—or Camelot. I just felt alone.

In Scotland during a meditation, I astral projected out of my body, flipped over and was shocked to be nose-to-nose with my own serene self. Shocked, I fell back into my physical body. I saw visions, heard voices and had psychic abilities, yet felt empty inside—the carrot continually dangled in front of my nose as I sought God.

Sitting in a cave on a cliff in Crete overlooking the Mediterranean Sea I gazed at the sky looking for a sign, looking for God. "Where are You?" I asked.

The more I travelled, the more desperate I became to have an encounter that not only gave me a spiritual thrill, but provided both peace and inner fulfillment. After six months visiting dozens of sacred sites in twenty countries I felt agitated and hopeless. God was not to be found in these places.

I sought God in the spectacular. I wanted an earth-moving experience to prove to me He was real. I'm reminded what the angels said to Mary Magdalene and the other women who sought the body of Jesus at the tomb after His crucifixion. *"Why do you seek the living among the dead? He is not here, but is risen!"* (Luke 24:5-6). I discovered there are no sacred sites magnetized to hold God's presence. He's just not there. But the "image of God" who walked on the earth nearly 2000 years ago is "risen" and His Holy Spirit will also indwell all who ask Jesus to reside on the throne of their hearts and be Lord of their lives. But these mysteries were hidden from me then.

The spectacular experiences, while they thrilled me for the moment, left me empty, agitated, and craving another 'fix.' Later, after I accepted a relationship with the Person of Jesus Christ, I discovered that my encounters with God could be sweet, profound, fulfilling— and the deep sense of peace His presence engenders remains.

A Dangerous Question

After my parents died, I decided to leave a so-so career as an actor in New York City for the seeming serenity of a New Age community in the Ozark foothills. "I'll go where I'm happy and start my life over again," I thought. Since I didn't find God in my travels to sacred sites, I hoped settling in a community centered on a person channeling an Ascended Master would bring me closer to the source of enlightenment.

Not surprisingly, the change of scenery did not change *me*. As the saying goes, "Wherever you go, there *you* are." The empty feelings and unhappiness followed me from New York City.

I was lonely. I wanted someone to love me for myself. In the end, it was the loneliness that brought me to my knees.

The first time I surrendered to God was the most difficult thing I'd ever done. Control has always been important to me. No one likes feeling helpless. When I became aware of my mother's psychological weaknesses as a child, I remember clenching my fists and saying to myself, "*I will never be weak. I will always be strong.*" It didn't work. I was a practicing alcoholic from the ages of 13 to 29.

In the spring of 1987 I was driving home to the New Age community where I lived, when a 'dangerous' question entered my mind. **"What if everything you thought about God was completely wrong. Would you be willing to give it up to know the Truth?"**

That question was dangerous because it led me to doubt what I thought I knew. I had a lot invested in the New Age and yoga—twenty-two years of my life. I was even being groomed to play a role as one of the spiritual leaders in the community where I lived.

That question in my mind begged an answer. "What if everything you thought about God was completely wrong. Would you be willing to give it up to know the Truth?" "If" was a big word.

"*If everything I thought about God was completely wrong,*" I said aloud. "*Would I be willing to give it all up to know the truth?*" Well, *if* I was wrong... "*Yes,*" I answered. Yes, I would be willing to give up everything I thought I knew about God in order to know the truth.

The next day I came to the end of myself.

The April Fool?

On April 1st I was alone with my border collie Tula in my little house on the mountain. I walked in circles around the kitchen for what seemed like hours. I called out to God.

From the depths of my being I cried, "*I surrender. I give up. You win. If you can do something with this life, You can have it.*"

I knew I was crying out to the Jesus of my childhood. I asked Him to forgive me for making such a mess of my life.

Between sobs I said, "*If You want me to be alone, then give me peace. If You want me to be with someone, then send him soon, because I can't live like this anymore.*"

I fell on my knees and then on my face. As I did, I felt a physical weight lift off me and something I'd never experienced before—peace like a dove came upon me and filled me. This peace was not the mind-numbing serenity I'd experienced during yoga meditations. It was not the blissful emptiness where nothing really mattered. I felt loved and embraced, accepted and fully, vibrantly alive.

The Peace I'd Been Missing

Peace. I'd never known how good it could feel. I never knew what peace was before. I'd always associated it with boredom or the words *"Rest in Peace"* on cartoon tombstones. This was different. From the center of this remarkable peace came joy. This joy I felt was not mere happiness or the giddy delight of opening presents. For the first time in my life I felt complete. Perhaps the best word for it is *shalom* in Hebrew—which means peace; wholeness; nothing missing, and nothing broken.

"For He Himself is our peace," the Apostle Paul wrote of Jesus in the New Testament (Ephesians 2:14). For me, His peace was the missing piece. I gave God everything I had, every mixed-up, messed-up part— and He gave me Himself: love, completeness and glorious, childlike joy.

The Jesus of my childhood, the One who laughed at my jokes was not a religion, but a Person. I never wanted to have a *religion*! I wanted a relationship—a relationship with God. That's what I'd been looking for all my life—to actually know God. I wanted to hear His voice, love Him—and know His love for me.

Oh, how I wished someone had told me sooner that I could have an actual relationship with God! Why did no one tell me that all the knowledge in the world could not equal one spark of revelation from God? By being willing to give up everything I thought I knew about God, I came to know the Truth. I learned that the Truth is not a debatable philosophy or mindset, but a Person: Jesus Christ. He said, "I am the way, the <u>truth</u> and the life. No one comes to the Father except through Me" (John 14:6).

That April Fool's Day I went from being a fool for the world, to a fool for Christ. I don't worry about looking or sounding foolish for sharing the love of Jesus. How I wish others had been willing to be that foolish when I was so lost and alone—imprisoned behind the wall of separation from God.

Shortly after I surrendered to God I realized I no longer had any desire to drink the bottles of Italian wine I used to consume on an almost daily basis since I was 13 years old. The desire was completely gone. In God's great mercy, He removed alcoholism with the weight He lifted off me.

Remember the prayer I prayed, *"If You want me to be alone, then give me peace. If You want me to be with someone, then send him soon..."*? Four days later, I met Paul Willis, and we were married three months later, on the 4th of July 1987 and have celebrated 23 years of bliss this past year.

I discovered that God will give you the desires of your heart when you delight yourself in Him.

God's Sense of Humor

God has a sense of humor—and He never wastes a thing in our lives. The gifts and natural talents I had since childhood have come to fruition and found fulfillment in my relationship with Him.

One of the reasons I left the theater in New York City was because of the emptiness I felt. The applause no longer satisfied me. Since then I've been blessed to present a number of original theater performances through our company, DoveTale Productions. Remember how the 'Ascended Master' rebuked me for my desire to serve others? I've heard that the word 'entertainment' comes from a Latin word which means *"to serve."* Entertaining others felt empty for years because I didn't feel I had anything worthwhile to share. Now I do. I no longer entertain to be served by others' handclaps and accolades, but because I finally have something meaningful to give.

Since 1993 I've presented one-woman shows and ensemble productions in theaters, schools, churches and community centers. I enjoy writing shows that bring history *'off the page'* in interactive ways for today's audiences.

I've also been amazed that my years in yoga have not been wasted either. We started a Fitness Ministry called PraiseMoves in 2003, and now have DVDs and books with Harvest House Publishers, two television shows for children and adults seen by over 250 million people globally, and Certified PraiseMoves Instructors on four continents bringing a Christ-centered alternative to yoga to communities around the world. Our website **www.praisemoves.com** has drawn millions of visitors.

Over 125 postures are each linked to a different verse from the Bible, as well as numerous "Scripture Sequences:" multiple postures that coincide with quoting longer passages like the 23rd Psalm or the Lord's Prayer.

Actually, I believe that physical exercise is not the foundation to PraiseMoves. The Scripture we meditate upon is the foundation. The exercise is the "witty invention" to get us more into the Word of God from the Bible, and to get more of the Word into us—hence our slogan, *"Transform your workouts into worship"* with PraiseMoves.

We even have a series of postures based on the shapes and meanings of the letters in the Hebrew alphabet (*alef-bet*). I studied the Kabbalah in the New Age, but this teaching is different—everything points to Jesus as Messiah! For example, the Hebrew word for religion is *"dat,"* which is a combination of the fourth letter of the alphabet *dalet* (which means "door") and the 22nd letter *tav* (which originally looked like a cross, or the lower case letter 't'—and held the meaning of "sign" or "cross"). So, the ancient Hebrew word for religion is "door of the cross." How remarkable is that?

The Center of My Joy

I thank God I found "the door of the cross" and walked through it. As I look back, I am grateful beyond words that I did not lose my life during one of the many alcoholic blackouts I had in my teens and twenties. I didn't lose my mind while dabbling in the supernatural, dallying in the psychic arena as if it were a sandbox; allowing my body to be used as a channel for strange spiritual forces, instead of a vessel yielded to God.

The God who laughed at my jokes and comforted me in the darkness of my closet has become the center of peace and light within my own heart. He has become the center of my joy! I would have never imagined that all the love, peace, wisdom and spiritual fulfillment I craved could be found in relationship with Jesus, the God of the Bible, the Living Word and Creator of the universe.

One day the Author of Love asked me a question, *"What if everything you thought about God was completely wrong. Would you be willing to give it up to know the Truth?"* I'm glad I answered yes to the Truth. How about you? What if...?

Laurette Willis is the founder/director of PraiseMoves, a popular, biblically based alternative to yoga. She has two PraiseMoves telecasts (one for children and one for adults) seen by a potential audience of over 250 million people globally, as well as certified PraiseMoves instructors on four continents. She lives in Tahlequah, Oklahoma, with her husband, Paul, who shares her vision of impacting the world with the Gospel of Jesus Christ.

Bottled Up...Broken...and...Poured Out!

By Correna Monroe

I accepted the Lord as my savior, at the age of 7. I was raised in a home where we went to church whenever the doors were open and I loved going. I loved the Lord with all of my heart and enjoyed learning about Him.

As I grew older, I started to become very confused because while I was taught not to do certain things, it was obvious that everyone around me (including my own family) were doing those "unheard" and wrong things. That is where the struggle began.

When I was 12, I was sent to a summer camp with my church. That summer, I learned about the importance of staying pure until marriage and I deeply wanted to please God so I made a commitment to wait for that special man He created for me. Everything in my life seemed to be going well and I was committed.

The summer after my freshman year, I was asked by my sister to sneak out and go with her to a party. Over and over I begged my sister not to go, but she would not listen. She wanted me to go so that her chances of getting in trouble if she were caught would be lessened. Mom would trust "our excuse" more if we were together. I broke and went along with her.

That evening I was with my sister, her best friend, and a guy that my sister liked. When we arrived at the party there were two boys there I had never met and they were smoking marijuana. It was offered to me several times and I did not partake in any of it. As for my sister, I cannot say for sure but she left the hotel room to hang out with her boyfriend and left me there with her best friend. As people began leaving the room where the party was being held, I realized that I would be left alone and started to leave to look for my sister. I was the last to leave except for this strange young man that kept bothering me and her friend all night long. As I went to leave, he slammed my arm in the door so I could not leave and brutally raped me. My sister eventually came back to the hotel room and found me. I blacked out and did not remember anything after the rape. I don't even remember how I left, I just remember lying in my bed and waking to my sister next to me saying she's so sorry.

For days I could not speak and did not tell anyone what happened because I wanted to protect my sister along with myself for "sneaking out". I felt dirty and useless and the feelings I had stuffed kept me withdrawn and unable to be myself. I was completely bottled up.

I remembered the promise I made to God to stay pure and now it was broken and I was broken. I blamed myself because I should never have had been there in the first place. Here I was bottled up, broken and not even a year later, I was raped again. This time it was not a stranger but it was by my sister's boyfriend! He was someone that I thought I could trust and someone I went to school with. I also thought of him like a brother.

I lost all trust in any male and even struggled being around my own father at times. After many years of remembering the past and lacking self-worth, I ended up in a relationship with someone who I had no intentions of marrying and did not trust. Like many women who have been betrayed by men, I no longer cared about being married, but I had a desire to have a child of my own to love, protect and make a difference in their life. I eventually gave in to have sex with him outside of marriage and prayed that I would get pregnant. While praying, I promised God that I would straighten out my life and raise a child for "Him" and soon became pregnant.

I was pregnant and he wanted nothing to do with the baby and asked me to get an abortion. After he realized there was no way I would have an abortion, we tried to stick together. He even considered getting married to do what was right but in the year my daughter was born, he became overwhelmed with all the responsibilities and endured many tragedies in his life. Instead of turning to God for help, he chose drugs and alcohol. Once again my distrust in men continued to grow and I just added him onto the list of the *"men"* I do not trust.

The last straw that broke the camel's back was the day the verbal abuse became physical and he threatened my life. That very day was when I picked my daughter up off the floor where she had been playing never to return again.

The promise I made to care, love and raise her for the Lord became easier to keep but there were times where I struggled financially and emotionally being a single mom. However, I would not trade those times for anything. Thankfully, I had many loving family members willing to help watch her while I worked to make a living for us.

Then the day came when I finally began to trust men again when I met Kirk (my husband). We became good friends and went to church together each Sunday. After months of a close friendship, we began dating and I fell in love with him. But, then I ran. I was scared to be hurt again even though he never did anything wrong. I purposely did not speak to him for three months and during that time I would pray that I would be able to have someone like him. So here I am running from the man that I know is the one for me while praying to God that He would send me a man just like Kirk? Sounds crazy doesn't it? The problem was that I believed the lies Satan told me. Satan kept whispering in my ear while I was dating Kirk that I was not good enough and I was dirty. After praying continually and Kirk praying for me, I was led back to him. We continued to go to church together and pray for our relationship.

Six months later, Kirk asked me to marry him and that is when the "purity" thing came in. Kirk listened and helped me through all of my insecurities about what happened to me and the mistakes I had made in my past while we were dating. He was and still is my best friend. I kept praying that God would make me pure for him, clean every dirty thing away from me, blot out my transgressions and heal every wounded part of my body and soul. I wanted my future husband to feel as though he was not cheated and was getting a pure wife and to see me as his true mate for life that God created just for him. Kirk prayed the same way and God showed up and answered our prayers by spiritually cleansing me before our marriage.

We waited to be intimate until we were married and to this very day, it made all the difference in our marriage. God restored me, made me pure again and today because of letting go of the *"secrets of my past"* (pouring out) has fully redeemed me completely! The chains are gone and I have been set free! Psalm 51:10, 12 (NIV) says *"Create in me a pure heart, O God, and renew a steadfast spirit within me... Restore to me the joy of your salvation and grant me a willing spirit, to sustain me".*.....God did just that and I am forever free and full of joy! Regardless of what you have been through or what Satan has lied to you about. Seek God, Trust God and BELIEVE that God can restore, redeem and give you back everything that the enemy has stolen from you.

If God can do it for me, He can do it for you! Now, it is with much joy that I pour out what He has given me to whomever I can. I am a willing vessel to share this for His glory!

Overcoming Depression – Learning to Live Again
By Patty Mason

If you are suffering from depression, I know how you feel. I know you are hurting emotionally, spiritually and physically. I know the sense of hopelessness and despair. I understand the isolation and the feelings of abandonment by others, even by those you once called friends. I know, more than anything, you long to end the madness and stop feeling like a prisoner in your own skin.

Depression was devastating, debilitating, destructive and demoralizing. It crippled my mind, heart, spirit and soul and destroyed every part of me. Nothing kept me held in a world of pain and suffering like depression. It was an unceasing vacuum that gripped my soul in such a way that it rendered me utterly helpless and hopeless. I couldn't control what was happening. My once energetic personality lost its drive. I felt drained and tired, and I lost all interest to do anything or go anywhere.

When the depression hit, I became confused and wondered why this was happening to me. Where did I go wrong? At the time, I was seemingly living a good life, a life that appeared to be full of hopes and dreams, plans and expectations. So what happened? How could the highest point of my life so quickly become the lowest point? It made no sense, but when the depression hit, my world came crashing down around me, and I didn't have the faintest idea how to begin to pick up the pieces, much less put my broken life back together.

Where Did I Go Wrong?

I remember the day I began to fall into the well of depression. I was standing on stage in Dallas, Texas, before an audience of thousands, being recognized for one of the highest levels of achievement in the company. My husband was in the audience, proud of the accomplishments I had attained. Yet, as I stood on that stage, surrounded by joyful celebration and shouts of praise, I found myself thinking: Is this all there is? Abruptly, everything I had poured myself into that year became worthless. As I stood on that stage, listening to the loud music and thunderous applause, I began to think to myself: Is this what I shipped my children off to a babysitter for? Is this what I did the changing of the guard with my husband for? In the middle of what should have been a magnificent moment, my soul began to plummet from that momentary high, to a miserable point of confusion.

On the flight home from the awards celebration, hot tears of frustration and anger welled up in my eyes. I was at the peak of success when I hit a wall and experienced a sense of loss that left me spiraling helplessly down a deep, dark tunnel.

In the days that followed the conference, I began to turn my back on everything and everyone I initially thought would bring me happiness. I found fault and became critical of everything my husband and children did, or didn't do. Nothing was good enough; and, no matter how hard my family tried to please me they couldn't gain my approval. And the career I once loved became pointless.

I wandered through each day like a blind beggar, not knowing what I was begging for. Nothing helped—no matter what I did in an attempt to feel better, it didn't work. I couldn't get over the overwhelming feelings of sadness and worthlessness. Each day became increasingly harder—every minute increasingly darker.

Hiding the Hurt, Masking the Pain

It was ironic, I was thirty-five years old and had everything this world deems valid. I had a husband who loved me, three beautiful healthy children, a nice home, and a successful career. I had achieved everything I set out to accomplish since I was 18-years-old. Yet, I was miserable.

Wasn't all of this success supposed to make me feel good? Wasn't it meant to give me some kind of worth and validate me as a person? I had a man, children, money, a career, yet none of it brought me the happiness and fulfillment I craved.

For a long time, I allowed a world that didn't have the faintest idea how to live, tell me how to live. I bought into the commercial. I believed the lie. I was sold on the concept that this is what a perfect life is supposed to look like. But once I had everything I had dreamed about, instead of experiencing happiness, feelings of discouragement flooded my soul.

What should have been my greatest journey toward satisfaction, turned out to be my worst nightmare. Nothing made me happy; nothing made me whole; nothing gave me the sense of life, love and purpose I was frantically searching for. In an attempt to find myself—I lost myself. I didn't have a clue where to turn. I didn't know where to look anymore.

Even though I was falling apart emotionally and spiritually, I didn't want to admit it. Admitting my inner (wo)man was a mess meant failure. Outwardly I had it all, so how could I tell others I was miserable? I believed the lie that I had to be great, self-reliant, and perfect, or at least look like I was perfect. It wasn't okay for me to look like I had a great life and then say, "I'm not okay;" at least, not out loud. So, I lied. I kept everything locked inside and pretended; when, in reality, I was nothing more than a perfect example of the walking wounded. I worked hard at wearing the mask of confidence, outwardly convincing those around me that nothing was wrong, when inwardly I was dying. I was nothing more than a living heart donor who was secretly screaming, "Help!" while wearing a smile. I was the true actor; a true veteran of the stage. Hollywood had nothing on me. I had my act down perfectly, so perfectly that no one could tell what was really going on in my life.

Struggling to Find a Way Out

I made every effort I could think of to find answers, to get better, to stop feeling the way I did; but nothing helped. With each attempt, failure was the only outcome. It was difficult for me to come to the conclusion I couldn't help myself, or free myself from the emotional turmoil. I had to look beyond myself in order to find relief. I had to open my heart and begin to tell people something was wrong, and I needed help. At first, I was afraid of what others would think. I wasn't sure how they would react when I told them about my depression. Would they judge me, criticize my actions and condemn my feelings? Would they stop loving me, or stop being my friend?

Up until this point, no one, not even my husband, knew about the pain I was going through. So, when I finally found the courage to start talking about the depression, to my surprise, no one judged, criticized or condemned. Instead, they simply didn't believe me. I was confused why no one took me seriously. I couldn't figure out why no one seemed to understand, or even listen.

I felt betrayed by the people I loved, so the love in my heart grew cold. I felt cheated, so I began to push people away. I didn't want to be around people who told me they loved me one minute, and then turned their backs on me the next. During the depression, I never felt lonelier. Even my sweet husband didn't get it. Almost every night I tried to tell him that something was wrong. And every time he would respond by saying, "Oh, you'll get over it." My husband loved me, I knew that, but he didn't understand what I was going through. He couldn't because he hadn't gone through depression himself, so he couldn't identify with the illness.

My husband telling me to "get over it," never helped me "get over it." I don't know why he made that assumption, other than the fact he simply didn't understand. My husband is usually the type of guy who wants to fix everything, and his way of fixing my problem was to tell me to "get over it." But, no matter how hard I tried, I couldn't. Believe me, if I could have controlled those overwhelming feelings of sadness and despair, I would have. What I needed from my husband was compassion. I needed an active listener who would give me an opportunity to be open and transparent, to really hear what I was experiencing. His lack of understanding made me feel even worse, and brought on feelings of hopelessness.

After I exhausted all efforts to find help through family and friends, I turned to the medical profession for relief. With phonebook in hand, I began to call one doctor's office after another; bent on the mission that if I could get some pills, I'd be fine. I had a get-fixed-quick mentality. I knew I needed help, and I figured a simple prescription would do the trick. So, that day, I went down the list, calling doctor after doctor, only to hear responses like: "I'm sorry, we don't take your insurance;" or, "I'm sorry, we don't handle that kind of depression."

In less than an hour, I had made my way through the entire list of professional doctors I thought could help me. Finally, when I dialed the last number on the list, a kind woman answered the phone and listened patiently to my heartfelt plea, only to tell me, at the end of our conversation, "I'm sorry, but we can't help you." As I hung up the phone a thought swiftly dawned on me: No one can help me—I'm utterly alone. This is never going to end. It was at that moment the darkness went deeper and thoughts of suicide entered my mind.

Hopelessness turned into utter desperation when I realized I was completely alone in my struggle. I had to do something to end the suffering. So I convinced myself that everyone would be better off without me. I knew committing suicide was wrong and my actions would hurt my family tremendously and leave a huge void in their lives; but, the darkness was so thick and heavy, I didn't see another answer. Death seemed to be the only way out of the darkness.

Turning Something Bad into Something Good

In the days that followed, I found myself doing something I very rarely did—I prayed. I did not pray for God's help, mercy, or healing. Nor did I call on him to find answers. Rather, I asked him to take my life. He had the power to make me live or die—and I wanted to die. Every morning I prayed for the insanity to end, and every night I prayed to never wake up. I would even lie down in the afternoons with that same prayer on my mind, Please, God, just let me die.

The most crucial point came on December 12, 1996. On this day I knew I couldn't go on one more day. When I awoke that morning, I felt my heart harden even more toward God for forcing me to face another day. I lay in bed, staring at the ceiling as if I were looking toward heaven and thought, Why won't you let me die?

Reluctantly, I got up and stepped into the shower. Hot tears began pouring from my eyes, mixing with the water pouring from the showerhead. Naked, drenched, and ashamed, I felt like I had been ground into the ashes from which I came. There was nothing left. I had reached the end of myself. And through the sobs, I began to talk to God. "I have nowhere else to go but You. You have to do something. No one can help me; only You can help me! Please, help me."

This was a completely different cry for relief and freedom. This time, I didn't ask him to end my life, I asked Him for much more. I asked for a miracle. I knew, as I cried out, this was a desperate make-it-or-break-it moment. If God didn't do something that day, I feared I would. My plea was not an ultimatum. I wasn't bargaining with God. I had hit rock bottom. I had nowhere else to go.

Suddenly, through the sobs, I heard what sounded like a faint voice, "Go to MOPS." (MOPS stands for Mothers of Preschoolers.) At first, I moaned. I didn't want to be around people. I didn't want to put on the mask again. As my emotions tried to persuade me to stay home, I heard it again, "Go to MOPS."

Once I arrived at the meeting, I immediately put on the mask that communicated to the world that I was doing fine. I was really struggling, but the last thing I wanted to do was let the ladies think I wasn't doing well. I didn't want them to know about the emotional turmoil, and I certainly didn't want them to know about my suicidal tendencies. It was just easier to pretend everything was okay.

Toward the latter part of our MOPS gathering, the speaker came forward and stood behind the podium. She shared about what it's like to have a lack of joy and no real purpose in life. She didn't specifically talk about depression, but what she was saying fell right in line with what I was feeling. The real crux of her message was about finding joy and purpose in life, and that the only way to find pure joy was through Jesus.

As she stepped from the platform, I watched her make her way to the back of the room. Without thinking, I got up and quickly made my way to the back. She looked at me and smiled warmly. Honestly, I don't remember how the conversation started, or how I got to the point of hysterics that I did, but before I knew it, I was dumping my life at her feet. Without warning, an emotional dam broke, and I found myself rambling and sobbing uncontrollably in front of her, trying desperately to form coherent sentences.

She didn't say a word as I continued to ramble through my frantic outburst. I couldn't control what was happening. I couldn't stop crying—and I couldn't stop talking—not even when I realized that every woman in the room had turned around to stare at us. Suddenly, I didn't care who knew, or what anyone thought. I needed help, and this woman had the answer. She seemed to understand even though she had never met me before. Somehow she knew what I was dealing with and wanted to help.

Quietly she listened for several minutes. Then, without saying a word, she reached out and touched me on my left arm; and when she did, the hysterics stopped. The crying and run-on sentences instantly stopped. There was no more nausea in the pit of my stomach. The dark cloud that had been my constant companion was gone. The heaviness lifted—everything—all of the darkness that had consumed my life was completely gone. My spirit and soul felt light, like they had taken on wings and could fly around the room. For the first time in my life, I felt free.

I was stunned and completely amazed. I stood there and stared at her, frozen by the event that had just taken place. At that moment, I had no idea if she knew or understood what had happened, because she still hadn't said a word. Yet, there was something about her I had never known before, and as I looked into her eyes, I could see great love and tender compassion. As I turned and walked away silently, my mind filled with thoughts as I struggled to comprehend the experience. I knew this woman did not possess the power to heal me, but

I believed God did. Even though I didn't fully understand what had happened, I was convinced the power I felt rush through me that day had to be God.

Finding Freedom

The week that followed, I was filled with nothing but joy. Instantly, my life rose from the darkness and burst with delight. Laughter and joy returned to my heart, and a sense of pleasure overtook my soul. A huge weight came off me the day I was delivered from depression. I was undeniably transformed, and everyone close to me noticed.

Another thing that happened was I couldn't stop thinking about Jesus. Prior to the depression I didn't know Jesus as my personal Savior, but since that day, He has changed my heart, old attitudes, and life in ways I never dreamed possible. He took all my striving, all my efforts to find happiness and self-worth, and offered me something of greater value. I went from looking for love—to knowing true love (1 John 4:16). I went from wearing the mask, trying to be perfect in a flawed world—to resting in the assurance that I am fearfully and wonderfully made (Psalm 139:14). I went from having no hope—to having a hope and a future (see Jeremiah 29:11).

God wanted me to be set free from the suffering; he just had another way of ending it. I thought the only way out was death, but God had other plans. When I saw only devastation in my life—God saw promise. When I saw only hopelessness—God saw a way to bring me near. To me the depression felt like the end—to God the depression was just the beginning of a whole new life with Him.

As a result of coming into a personal relationship with Jesus, my life has purpose; a true sense of determination that is leading me down paths I never dreamed I would take. For example, if you told me, prior to the depression, I would one day be an author and speaker, and be involved in women's ministry, I probably would have laughed. Even though I didn't see myself this way, God did. He knew the plans He had for me long before I was born. He knew what He desired to accomplish in my life, and He knew the path I would have to take to find my way to those purposes. From the beginning, God knew how to win my heart, draw me close to Him, and bring me into the plans He had for me.

Discovering Fresh Purpose and Life

I am living proof God can and will redeem a harmful past in order to give a bright future. At my lowest point, God came into the turmoil of my personal madness and set me free from depression. And when He set me free, He gave me a miraculous and powerful testimony—a testimony of hope, of love and deliverance, of healing power and his unfathomable grace.

God has a plan for your life, too. Sometimes, when you have been through so much, it's hard to wrap your mind around the reality that God loves you and has a purpose for your life.

God cares about you. He watches over you, and longs for the moment you will give your heart to Him. He sees your pain. He knows every tear you cry—and He knows the longing of your soul to find freedom. He wants to set you free and fill your heart with His love, fill all the empty places, so you have something to celebrate. He wants to redeem your past and give you a powerful testimony—to give you hope for the future.

Allow God to take your pain, turn it around, and use it. In the midst of your circumstances, God says, "I choose you." Not in spite of your past, but because of it. God wants to take all your emotional pain, redeem it, restore it, and use it—not only for His glory, but for the encouragement and support of others who are still suffering, too.

Embracing the Miracle

Through my life altering experience, I have learned a great deal. This is not to say that I have it all figured out, but what my experience has shown me is the truth behind what the speaker shared that day at the MOPS meeting. The only pure joy is in Jesus. She continued to reach out to me over the years; in fact, we are still friends to this day. Sue and I talked one day about what happened on December 12, 1996, but at that moment, she had no idea what God had done through her. She told me that she wondered why the ladies at MOPS even asked her to speak since she didn't have any children of her own. She told me that she had prayed for several days with a friend about what to talk about, since she felt she didn't have any motherly advice to give.

The first time Sue learned of the miracle God had done through her was at the MOPS Appreciation Night. It was about six months after the healing, and I was sharing my testimony publicly for the first time. After I shared my story, I turned to hand the microphone to the MOPS President, only to realize she was sobbing. She never took the microphone from me. Instead, she stood up, buried her face in my shoulder and wept. As I held her, I looked out at the audience and suddenly realized everyone was crying. Then, I saw Sue, she, too, was weeping as she made her way to the front of the sanctuary. For several minutes, the three of us held each other, embracing the hope and the miracle that was given to all of us by a merciful and glorious God.

God wants to heal and restore you, too. He wants you to be free from depression; but, it is important to understand that God is sovereign. The way He chooses to deliver you from this pain, and the time frame in which He chooses to release you, is completely in His hands. God is a God of miracles. As in my case, He can reach out and heal you in an instant. However, please recognize God's primary purpose is to bring wholeness, to bring you close to Him, so He may not heal you the same way He healed me. But be assured, He can do anything, if you give Him the opportunity.

Therefore, reach out to Jesus. Take off the mask. Invite Him into all the areas of your brokenness by acknowledging your need for Him. Open your heart and ask Him to give you hope. Ask Him to help you overcome depression, and teach you how to live in Him.

Story taken from *Finally Free: Breaking the Bonds of Depression Without Drugs,* By Patty Mason. To order your copy or to learn more about Patty and Liberty in Christ, visit www.LibertyinChrist.net

Unconditional Love

By Rosemary Fisher

As a girl growing up I struggled with the concept of unconditional love or even the idea of a heavenly Father who loved me with all my flaws, hang ups and bad habits. The reason why I struggled believing was because my "earthly" father modeled the exact opposite. I never heard my father tell me that he loved me, that I was beautiful or worth fighting for. My father never expressed any interest at all in learning what my gifts were or what made my heart sing.

My father was the problem parent who always engaged in some form of immature, inappropriate, or destructive behavior which was a detriment to our entire family. He drank daily (unless he had a major hangover), used foul language, and physically and mentally abused my mother and our entire family due to his alcoholic addiction and fits of rage and anger. This did not happen on occasion but for the majority of my childhood.

My mother on the other hand was a passive parent who allowed this inappropriate behavior to continue, which always left me and my older brother in dangerous situations. Her self-esteem and self-worth was so low that she continuously allowed my father to break her down and control and manipulate her to believe that it was all her fault for the broken relationship and violence within our family.

I witnessed the love my mother would put forth to please my father and because she would not stick up for herself or protect us from my father, I grew to despise and resent her weakness as a woman. This is when the trouble began in my spirit. I began making silent vows within my soul to NEVER allow a man to control my life, like my father controlled her and our family.

Although my family life was a mess, I had no choice but to grow accustomed to the constant chaos. I loved both of my parents and wanted nothing more than to have a "happy" home life. It was my heartbeat and desire to be loved and for them to love each other. I would continue to pray and wish that one day I would hear those precious words to every story I read as a little girl... *"and they lived happily ever after"*.

Mother took us to church and did her best to instill spiritual beliefs in us. Unfortunately, my father was aligned with a different church with conflicting theology which caused more confusing competition. I was in love with God and wanted Him to love me back by protecting me. I wanted God to rescue me and my family from all the pain our family was enduring and was willing to do whatever God wanted me to do to fix this.

The more I jumped on my father's back to release my mother or my brother from my father's clutches, the more scared, insecure and angry I became. I continued to resent my mother's weakness for not leaving and my brother vented his anger on me and vice versa. Not only did I feel resentment toward my mother but I began questioning the validity of our church as well. Along with gossip about our family was a passive resignation toward the black eyes Mother often wore on Sundays. And another thing: Why was I hearing what the Bible taught about certain behaviors and then seeing the church folks acting in opposite ways during the week? What kind of religion is that? Not anything I wanted. I wanted REAL!

I was nine years old when my father died suddenly on his thirty-third birthday. He was fatally hit by a tractor-trailer full of his favorite comfort drink: beer. To his credit, my mother was able to sustain our lifestyle after his death because he had always been a wonderful provider in a material way.

His funeral was my first and as the casket lowered into the ground the finality of things hit me hard. He was gone. It was over and I would never have a chance to hear from his lips that I was loved, beautiful, captivating and worth fighting for. I was broken not knowing how to pick up the pieces. Only later in life did I understand that he had no idea how to love his family or to share his heart. His father had acted the same toward his family, a repeated pattern that became a generational curse.

We were now free from the physical and verbal abuse, but the freedom mentality also brought much destruction along with it. Since my mother hated the control that my father had on her and our family, she thought it was best to make it up to me by not having any boundaries on my life which left me wide open to do what I wanted and when I wanted. I lost all respect for authority and stepped into the role of being my own authority since my mother relinquished her responsibility. I quit school in the eighth grade and got involved with a rough crowd in our neighborhood.

Over a short period of time I lost interest in being a fourteen year old honor roll student who was active in sports and horseback riding and decided hanging out in bars with my mother was more important than my grades or sports. Church had to go, too. What use were those who put on a big front once a week, only to become someone different during the week? My friends would at least be real and genuine, even if their lives were a mess. A new disgust for church and all it stood for had settled deep within my heart.

As my mother continued her "party" lifestyle, she became extremely depressed and soon after my sixteenth birthday, she committed suicide and left me and my brother to fend for ourselves. She believed that I was strong enough to handle life on my own and did not need her anymore. We were devastated.

The shock of finding her dead only intensified my disbelief that there was a God that was loving and kind. The only person who I trusted that loved me chose to leave me. Not for a little while, but forever! The memory of trying to bring her back to life and begging her not to leave me seems as if it was yesterday. The thought of it being my fault would replay over and over in my heart and mind. *Why did I leave her and start hanging out with other girlfriends? Why didn't I hang out more at home? Why didn't I watch her more carefully? Why did I treat her with such disrespect? Why? Why? Why?* The only cure for the constant battle within my mind was to kill the pain and voices with alcohol and bad relationships.

The day she died, her *"religious"* family came over to claim what they thought was theirs. While sitting in my living room chair in shock over her death praying that I would wake up to discover that I was in a bad nightmare, I could hear her family in the kitchen talking amongst each other saying *"Mary told me I could have this... Mary told me I can have that"*. As I continued to hear them casting lots for my mother's belongings, the anger festered within my entire being to the point of chasing each one of them out of our home.

Because of not having a *"healthy"*, *"secure"* or *"protective"* environment, I didn't know how to have healthy relationships with my family, friends or people in authority. I was impaired emotionally, psychologically and spiritually. I continued to have false ideas of who God was and the enemy was ready and willing to feed me plenty of lies along the way. Remember, I made internal vows to never trust a man or allow a man to control my life and this is when the rebellion began to bear fruit in my life.

With no one left to count on, no one anywhere worthy of my trust, the thing left to do was to run and kill the pain with alcohol, drugs and lethal relationships. Looking back, I was becoming everything I hated. I was turning into my father in spite of vowing years earlier that I would NEVER act like him.

A current pop song on the radio was, "Running with the Devil." The enemy used the power of music as an invitation to give my life to him and to lose my faith in a loving God. As the song played I announced, *"If God is so mean to take away everything I love... I would rather run with the devil!"* That day I opened the door for my life to become a living hell.

And run with the devil I did — with a hell-bent mission to crash and burn in a flame of glory. After years of drinking, drug use, sick relationships and a failed marriage, I lost all desire to continue on until I met a very special friend. A friend who loved me more than my mother ever knew how.

Her name was Christine Petros and we were introduced by a mutual business contact that knew we would work well together because Chris was a clothing designer and I had a modeling agency. We were instant friends and God with His divine wisdom knew she was the only woman who could run with me that I would respect because of her strength and her talents that overshadowed mine. She immediately took lead role as my older sister, sticking with me through my wild escapades and off-the-edge drinking bouts. She also witnessed my first time falling in love with a man I knew was too good for me.

Well versed in the disease of alcoholism due to family involvement, she easily recognized what I wanted to hide. Alcohol was my master; I had no power to overcome the addiction or had a replacement to cover the pain that was so deep ingrained within my heart and soul. But Chris had seen the other side of the alcohol story. She knew there was deliverance and healing — from the proper source. The moment of truth came on a long drive home one night when she turned to me with teary eyes, announcing, *"If you don't stop this lifestyle, you are going to die and I can't watch it anymore. I love and care about you and either you allow me to get you help, or you will need to find another business partner and friend. I can no longer watch you destroy yourself"*.

When Chris spoke, she delivered. A "mover and a shaker" type, she got things done ... and she meant business. I understood the challenge: Allow my best friend to get me meaningful help, or lose her forever. What kind of love this was — or where it originated I could not imagine. With a melted heart, I was ready because for the first time in my life I had someone who loved me enough to tell me the truth.

I never experienced someone truly concerned about my welfare or well being. She was the first friend I ever had that was willing to be that voice to speak truth into my life in hopes that I would choose life instead of death.

The next day Chris picked me up and took me to my first Alcoholics Anonymous (AA) meeting. It was a strange and scary door to walk through. It was a Holy Spirit door where He began the work on my heart and in my life.

God knew I was adamant about not stepping a foot back into church because of those hypocrites. So God sent me where I needed to go and He was ever so present because where His people are, so is He.

While I attended AA meetings, I heard testimonies of people just like me. People who even did worse things than I did, yet they were happy, free and full of life! I noticed that they all had something in common that I did not have. They had "Jesus" as their Higher Power and were in "relationship" with Him. *I thought...Jesus! Jesus as a Higher Power?*

This wasn't any kind of Christianity I'd ever heard of. And this wasn't the Jesus I understood from childhood. In my thinking God and Jesus were mean-spirited dictators who could never be pleased. I was always on the wrong side of them. They were like my father, unpredictable and impossible to please. Right?

Wrong! I knew my problems were bigger than I was and it was either going to be life or death for me. I knew I could not fix myself because I tried every "new age" belief system, "self-help guru" and bought books and tapes on positive thinking and meditation. It would work for a short period of time only to find myself back once again in the pit of Hell repeating old habits and self-sabotaging behaviors.

Although I made a committed vow never to darken the church doors again it was no accident that all of the AA meetings were held in church basements or sanctuaries. Ironically, after experiencing God's love through other people and having found hope of the many testimonies I heard of a new found freedom, I would find myself many times trying to find a church that was open during off hours just to get in to seek who God was and try to find Him. I reached a point where the doors were locked at so many churches, that I would hang on the door, asking God to let the sinner in!

I wish I could tell you that I had a perfect scorecard for sobriety in the beginning and that I did not have to start over a few times because of relapsing. Those failures were lessons that taught me how desperately I needed a Savior that possessed the power that I did not have. It was that day that forever changed my life when I surrendered and dedicated my life to Christ Jesus as my Lord and Savior.

I will forever cherish that day when falling on my knees on my living room floor that I cried out to the Lord for His help and to save me. I told Him I no longer wanted to live this way and I was completely powerless over my life and situation. With a broken and contrite heart, a healing peace enveloped my entire spirit right then and there. With His forgiveness I began an inner transformation, like moving from the dark cocoon of a caterpillar to the freedom of a soaring butterfly! On that day everything looked brighter, like blinders had fallen from my eyes. I became hungry for truth, hungry to live, hungry to take responsibility for my choices and most of all a hunger to get to know and have a personal relationship with my heavenly Father.

God sent my best friend Christine to love me until I learned to love myself. He sent Christine to speak the truth into my life with love and concern. He sent Christine to set the example of how Christians are to serve others and how we are to love one another that draws them to Christ Jesus, not repels them. He used her love and concern to draw me into His loving arms and back to His church.

Yes, I am back in church, but for totally different reasons. I am no longer focused on taking everyone's inventory but concerned with what Jesus will say to me when I see Him face to face. He will not ask me about others, but will ask me what I have done for His kingdom. I come to church to worship my heavenly Father, to fellowship and learn the Word of God so I can live it and help others. It is my desire to love "unconditionally" as Christ loved me and how Christine showed me in the flesh. I always have to remind myself that no church denomination is perfect and that the church will always be filled with hurting people who are looking for the Christine's with Christ in them to serve them, love them where they are at and hear true testimonies of how God worked in their lives to give them hope for their futures.

God truly is a redeemer, restorer and repairer of damaged lives and circumstances. I made a choice to follow God and renounced the stronghold that the devil had on my life by the choice I made. I repented and have been forgiven. I have many stories and scars to show the destructive life that I led for many years that would take up this entire book. I have a testimony of what a mess looks like that is no different than yours. A mess is a mess regardless of how big or small it is. By God's grace I chose to come to Him and received His spirit for a new life. My lost childhood, deceased parents and lifestyle scars all bear witness that He was who I needed all along. He is who my entire family needed, even the very religious ones. God has walked me through layers of forgiveness toward my father, my mother and myself. He walked me through laying down the old and taking up the new.

By the way, that man I fell in love with (the one I thought was too good for me) became my husband more than fifteen years ago. We serve Jesus Christ together as best friends. We have an incredible twelve-year-old son who is blessed to live in a Christ-centered home where love and respect prevail. He knows we are not perfect, but that we are the same inside and outside our home.

Recycled Women was founded by God but given to me to lead women to share their stories of transformation and to challenge them to find God's very best for their lives. I pray that one day you will take joy in telling your story so that you can give God all the glory for His work of grace in you.

It is never too late! God is available and willing to intercede at any time to help you. Never forget that it does not matter how we begin, it only matters how we finish. I invite you to lay down the past and start a new, vibrant and loving relationship with your Creator. Whether you were like me and have never been asked to accept Jesus Christ as your Lord and Savior or you have backslidden and need to repent and get right with God. Either way, I have included at the back of this book a prayer of salvation as an example if you want to give up an ordinary life for an extraordinary life with eternal benefits! I believe in you and am praying for you!

Therefore, if anyone is in Christ, he is a new creation; old things have passed away; behold, all things have become new. 2 Corinthians 5:17 (NKJV)

Rosemary is the Founder of Recycled Women Ministries, LLC. For more information on how to share your story or information on the ministry, please visit **www.recycledwomen.org**

SPECIAL BOOK FEATURE....

Excerpt from the Men's Transformational Series...coming soon to a bookstore near you...

Witchcraft to God's Warrior

By Gary Beckstedt

By the age of twelve, I was living with my father, smoking mari-juana and Marlboro Reds, while cruising for willing girls every chance I could. Dad kept us in church every Easter and Christmas, quoted Corinthians every time his wife disagreed with him, and ruled his house with an iron fist. During the day, my brother and I would play 'Dungeons and Dragons' to get away from the emotional and physical abuse, leading to an addiction of running from reality through fantasy that would last for years. At night I would sneak downstairs to watch the Playboy channel while everyone else slept.

The summer I turned thirteen my mother received custody of me and my younger sister, splitting the three children up. It was a horrific time of lies and deceptions as both Mom and Dad used every means at their disposal to hurt the other through us kids. When the dust settled, I was in Texas with my mother and didn't speak to my Dad again for two years.

It was July when a local neighbor kid approached me about some-thing called 'VBS'. Little did I know what was going on when I rode with him to a church near our house. A large group of kids were there, and we played, ate, and sang songs I had never heard before. As the day drew to a close, one of the adults came into the room where we were all seated and began to tell the story of Jesus. By the point of the crucifixion I was in tears. I remember being led into another room to say a prayer. The only thing I remember about that event was asking Jesus to come into my heart. Someone gave me a bible and I started to read.

My mother had no interest in being a part of my new life. My step-father made it clear that if I wanted to attend a church that it was my business. He, on the other hand, would have none of it in his house. So I attended by myself in my yard sale clothes, with my 'poor white trash' lifestyle, and started to learn how to love God. I became very hungry for the Word of God but when I went to Sunday school and asked so many questions I was told to be quite.

The church had a small private school and every Sunday the Pastor would petition the congregation for more money to keep the school open and it did. One Sunday morning, the lesson was on the world, and how things were going in it. That morning, my whole hope of salvation was dashed with the words, *"If your kids are in a public school instead of our private school, you are sending them to Hell."* I knew that there was no way my parents would find the money to send me to this private school so in my thirteen year old logic, I made the decision that if I was going to Hell anyhow, I might as well make the best of it. And so I did....

Like most teenagers, I spent most of my time thinking about the opposite sex. The biggest difference between me and 'them' was the single-mindedness I had concerning sex. It was all I could think about, and thoughts of perversion dominated my mind. I found myself getting interested in every depraved and ungodly act I could find. In the midst of all this, I met a girl who would have nothing to do with me. I became completely obsessed with her, and determined in my mind that I would do anything to get her.

Sin is a magnet to other sinners, and in this case, a powerful one. I met another girl in school who claimed to be a witch. She explained that she could perform a spell for me that would absolutely get me the girl I wanted. I did all the things she required of me, and within three weeks the girl was mine.

Immediately I was no longer interested in the girl, sex or drugs but this 'power of witchcraft' that could change the very desires of men. I thought, *"If I could master something like this, no one would be able to hurt me ever again."* Every available moment was spent digging into books and articles about witchcraft. I wanted to understand it, use it and master it. Little did I see that it began to master me.

Within one year while I was in my Junior year of High School, I felt like I was getting good at "*The Craft*" and discovered the science of Demonology. I dove headlong into this discipline, buying books, attending ceremonies and absorbing everything I could get my hands on. I began to discern the difference between charlatans and real demons. And for once, I began to fear. I began to see that Hell is for real and that demons can possess people, and could kill them at will.

A young man introduced me to a particularly demonic tome full of spells and curses. He warned me that after reading this book, he had begun to have terrifying nightmares and could hear demons talking to him at night. Skeptically, I began studying and practicing some of the spells myself. All that came to a halt within a month when this same young man was arrested for attempting to kill his mother with a kitchen knife. I spoke to him later, and he shared with me that he had been wrestling with the demons who kept telling him to kill his mother. The night of the attack he said that he lost consciousness and had no recollection of the events whatsoever. While the legal and medical fields dismissed this as a mental health issue, I knew better. Now I was gripped with fear and wanted to learn how to protect myself and gain mastery over these invisible forces.

After graduation, I moved to Georgia to live with my father and to escape the dominion of my mother. There were also some of the most powerful cults in America in the Atlanta area. I immediately linked into a group of Wiccans that taught me how to read Tarot cards, how to release my spirit from my body through what is known as Astral projection, and a variety of curses and blessings that I could command. At last, I found people who were convinced they could command and control the demonic forces I had already seen in action. But they were so wrong. Rather than control these forces, they were used by them to seduce others into this deception. With each passing hour, we sought deeper and deeper extremes of depravity and power.

My life continued to slide into decadence and depravity. Every new experience was to be desired and every taboo to be explored. Each day found me looking for something new to try. I began reading books about Satanic worship and Hedonism. I left the perceived safety of witchcraft and began going even deeper into Hell. By the time the summer ended, I had found the writings of a man who taught Satanic worship without the distasteful sacrifice of children and animals. Instead, he glorified the flesh while acknowledging the need of man for spiritual food. His arguments were compelling, and sinfully delicious. As an 18 year old male, with no meaningful discipline in his life, all this fit in quite nicely with the desires I spent every evening fulfilling.

I started to become bored and decided that what I needed was another change in my life so I enlisted in the military and was shipped out in 1989. While in basic training, I remembered someone I had left behind several years ago.

One aspect of basic training is the Sunday morning service to help new soldiers adjust to their new lifestyles. It is not mandatory to attend but if you don't, you can stay behind and clean the dorms and for this reason, you can understand why they are so popular. It was because of this need for a break that I found myself walking into a church. It seemed silly to me, almost ironic, that a servant of Satan could walk into this sanctuary in sheep's clothing. I could not explain the pit in my stomach, so I dismissed it as breakfast. But sometime during the choir's singing of "*Amazing Grace*", conviction washed over me and I found myself on my knees, begging God to have mercy on me. All the scriptures I had forgotten came rushing back in like tidal waves.

For the remainder of Basic Training, I was faithful to attend church every Sunday, but because I had no Christian support system in place, as soon as I was released back into the world I went back to the vomit I knew.

Over the next seven years, my life fell into a slide of hate and misery. My self esteem fell to a point where suicide was not an "*if*" but a "how" and turned to alcohol to dull the emptiness in my life.

I married a girl from the area where I was stationed, and promptly began to ruin her life as well. Neither of us had any kind of spiritual foundation to base a marriage on. Instead we floundered through the days trying every pop psychological idea that was hot at the time. I introduced her to all the mysticism that I had learned over the years, and together we searched desperately for meaning and purpose in life.

A long season of financial strain, spiritual darkness, and relational ups and downs nearly ended our marriage. Just before we were to separate, however, Tina became excited about a new business opportunity – one that I, too, became curious about.

I went to a meeting with her to check it out and just as I had thought, it was an Amway meeting. But unlike the other times I had been to one of these things, this time seemed different. Intrigued by this feeling, I agreed to check things out and attend their upcoming convention. The money wasn't there for one of us to go, let alone both, but somehow I ended up going. I knew that many of the folks were Christians, and suspected that there would be plenty of brainwashing going on. I also assumed that my mind was girded up enough to keep me from making any emotional decisions.

The convention was three days long with a Sunday morning service taking place before the wrap up speakers. During that service, the Holy Spirit came back to visit. I was standing in respect of those around me, when an understanding of Jesus' death came into my mind. I saw Him hanging on the cross, His blood flowing. I felt the wall around my heart shatter, and ran to the floor of the arena to join the altar call. On July 7, 1996 I made a decision that stuck. This time, supported by a family of believers that helped me grow and understand, the decision was backed by more than just tears. I now had a support network that I could ask questions of, and fall back to when things got hard.

And the son said unto him, Father, I have sinned against heaven, and in thy sight, and am no more worthy to be called thy son. But the father said to his servants, Bring forth the best robe, and put it on him; and put a ring on his hand, and shoes on his feet: And bring hither the fatted calf, and kill it;

and let us eat, and be merry: For this my son was dead, and is alive again; he was lost, and is found. And they began to be merry. Luke 15:21-24 (KJV)

Giving my life to Christ during the convention did not make all my problems go away. There would be many years of sanctification, transformation, and deep healing to come for both my wife and myself. But the direction of our lives was definitely new. My heart was now in the hands of my Heavenly Father instead of in the clutches of the father of lies. Years of Christian relationships and godly wisdom through church fellowship continue to change my life. I've most definitely come a long way since my days of tarot cards and witchcraft.

I was praying one day about the pain of being so broken and of the suffering and turmoil that my life as one of "God's Warriors" has brought. The Lord showed me a vision that day of a beautiful pedestal that held two vases. The first vase was perfect, with delicate unbroken curves and intricate colors painted in magnificent patterns. I saw oil being poured into this vase until it was completely full. The oil licked at the edges at the top of the vase, but none spilled out.

The second vase was the opposite of the first. It had obviously been dropped and broken at some point, and while it had been glued back together there were pieces missing and excess glue flowed from the cracks. As I saw the oil about to be poured into this shattered vessel I already knew that the oil would go to waste as the vase would not be able to contain it. However, as I watched the expected results take place, I saw for the first time that many other vases were arranged around the base of the pedestal! As the oil flowed through the cracks and holes of the broken vase it filled the others as well!

The Lord said to me that day, "*You are that broken vase. The other vase, though perfect to look at, can only be filled with enough oil for itself. After that, the oil it has is all it will ever know. But you, in your brokenness, will not only share the oil that flows through you... BUT you will also see never ending streams of fresh oil as you will never be full. I did not cause you to be broken, but I did cause you to be healed. I did not restore you to what you were before your brokenness, but rather for the brokenness to remake you into something greater.*"

Living the Transformed Life Begins with the Free Gift of Salvation

My prayer is that these stories touched you in such a powerful way that you have a strong desire to have a relationship with your Lord and Savior. It does not matter where you are at in life right now, it only matters how you finish. I encourage you to finish well and become *"Recycled and Transformed"* for God's glory!

Today you can surrender your old life for an extraordinary life! There are no hidden tricks or agendas, just a sincere heart! God wants you to receive His free gift of salvation through His Son, Jesus Christ. Are you ready? If so... let's pray....

Father, You loved the world so much You gave Your only begotten Son to die for our sins so that whoever believes in Him will not perish, but have eternal life. Your Word says we are saved by grace through faith as a gift from You and there is nothing we can do to earn salvation.

I believe in my heart and confess with my mouth that Jesus Christ is Your Son, My Savior and the Savior of the world. I believe He died on the cross, bore all of my sins and You raised Him from the dead.

I confess Jesus as my Lord and Savior and ask that you forgive my sins and fill me up with Your Holy Spirit. Thank you for loving me enough to give Your very best for my salvation. In Jesus' holy name I pray, AMEN!!

The transformation begins right here! You have been given the gift of eternal life and the Spirit of Christ Jesus is residing in your heart!

Ask the Holy Spirit to help you find a church that teaches the Word of God so you can learn and grow. Also find a women's bible study to meet other Christian sisters to help you along the way. Don't be shy! True Sisters of Christ want to celebrate with you and will welcome you with open arms! If that does not happen, keep moving until you find the place where God wants you to be.

It is important for you to understand that it takes awhile to get what the inside has on the outside, so be patient and partner with God by reading and studying the Holy Bible as He begins to transform you from a caterpillar into a beautiful butterfly!

If this book has touched your heart in anyway, please share your story on our website at **www.recycledwomen.org**

Scriptures:
John 3:16 (NIV)
For God so loved the world that he gave his one and only Son, that whoever believes in him shall not perish but have eternal life.

Ephesians 2:8-9 (NIV)
For it is by grace you have been saved, through faith—and this is not from yourselves, it is the gift of God— not by works, so that no one can boast.

Romans 10:9-10 (NIV)
If you declare with your mouth, "Jesus is Lord," and believe in your heart that God raised him from the dead, you will be saved. For it is with your heart that you believe and are justified, and it is with your mouth that you profess your faith and are saved.

1 Corinthians 15:3-4 (NIT)
I passed on to you what was most important and what had also been passed on to me. Christ died for our sins, just as the Scriptures said. ⁴ He was buried, and he was raised from the dead on the third day, just as the Scriptures said.

1 John 1:9 (NKJV)
If we confess our sins, He is faithful and just to forgive us our sins and to cleanse us from all unrighteousness.

1 John 4:14-16 (NLT)

Furthermore, we have seen with our own eyes and now testify that the Father sent his Son to be the Savior of the world. All who confess that Jesus is the Son of God have God living in them, and they live in God. We know how much God loves us, and we have put our trust in his love. God is love, and all who live in love live in God, and God lives in them.

1 John 5:1 (NIV)

Everyone who believes that Jesus is the Christ is born of God, and everyone who loves the father loves his child as well.

1 John 5:12 (NIV)

Whoever has the Son has life; whoever does not have the Son of God does not have life.

1 John 5:13 (NIV)

I write these things to you who believe in the name of the Son of God so that you may know that you have eternal life.

COMING SOON....

RECYCLED WOMEN

SPIRITUAL BOOT CAMP

TRANSFORMATIONAL

STUDY

WARNING... THIS STUDY IS NOT FOR WIMPS... Spiritual Boot Camp is only for those women who want to experience God's transformational power in their life. This study guarantees RESULTS! **SPECIAL OFFER BELOW...**

Recycled Women Ministries

*Recycled Women will Captivate your Heart
While Refreshing your Soul......*

Recycled Women are available for your next conference, women's event or group coaching!

Need a Speaker? Want to put on your own Women's Event and need help? Invite Recycled Women to speak at your next upcoming event. We are here to serve you and are able to meet your specific needs. Just let us know your theme and we will help you make the match!

CONFERENCE, WORKSHOP AND SEMINAR TOPICS INCLUDE:

Blessing Ceremonies for Girls and Women, Caterpillar to a Butterfly, Shake Those Shackles Off Your Feet, Friendship Under Fire, Spiritual Boot Camp, How to Fight the Battle and Win, The Power of Words, How to Walk in FAVOR, Blessing Ceremony, How to Decorate your Cocoon and Love it, Personal Testimonies to fit any topic.... and MORE...

Recycled Women Ministries are here to share the transformational power of Jesus Christ through various true stories that will encourage, strengthen and validate the word of God.

Email us with your questions or needs at recycledwomen@gmail.com

Recycled Women Speaking Tour

Recycled Women Ministries is available for your next conference, women's event or group coaching! We respectfully minister in all denominations and are here to serve you! Contact us today!

What Ministry Leaders are saying about RWM:

Rosemary, what an awesome day we had with you at the Sullivan Baptist Women's conference. We have received so many positive comments. Your beautiful and inspiring presentation on God's saving grace and transforming power allowed all the women to lay their burdens at the feet of Jesus. The Holy Spirit was there and I thank you for being obedient to his call. God is so Good!... *Dawn Adcox, Women's Ministry Director, Sullivan Baptist Church*

"What an awesome experience and blessing it was to have the Recycled Women's Ministry at our church. The power of the testimonies of these beautiful women and what God has done in their lives was life changing for all who were there. May the Lord continue to bless this Ministry. I look forward to having them come again in the near future".... *Allison Rolston, Church of the Good Shepherd Episcopal Church*

The Women's Ministries Department of the Church of God of Prophecy in Tennessee was blessed to have "Recycled Women Ministries" as part of their annual 2010 Ladies Retreat. The enthusiasm and testimonies of Rosemary Fisher and Kristin Jordan had a profound effect upon those attending. Eternity only can reveal the power of "The Blessing".... *Londa Richardson, Church of God of Prophecy*

Contact us TODAY at www.recycledwomen@gmail.com

Made in the USA
Charleston, SC
07 July 2011